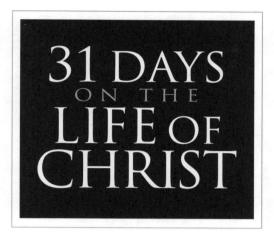

31 DAYS
ON THE
LIFE OF
CHRIST

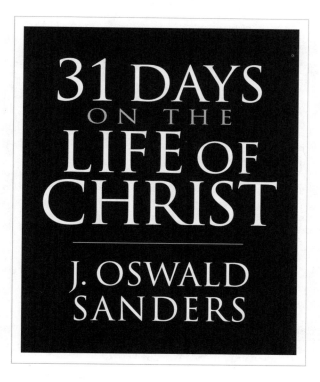

31 DAYS
ON THE
LIFE OF
CHRIST

J. OSWALD
SANDERS

MOODY PRESS

CHICAGO

Library of Congress Cataloging-in-Publication Data

Sanders, J. Oswald (John Oswald), 1902–
    31 days on the life of Christ / J. Oswald Sanders ; edited by James S. Bell, Jr.
     p. cm.
    Rev. ed. of: The incomparable Christ. 1971.
    ISBN 0-8024-5249-3
    1. Jesus Christ--Person and offices. I. Title: Thirty-one days on the life of Christ.
II. Bell, James S. III. Sanders, J. Oswald (John Oswald), 1902– Incomparable Christ.
IV. Title.

BT202 .S225 2001
232--dc21

2001032653

1 3 5 7 9 10 8 6 4 2

Printed in the United States of America

CONTENTS

PREFACE

W hat kind of man is this?" was a question frequently asked during the earthly ministry of Christ. His wise and challenging words and His incredible works demanded an explanation. The same question is still being asked today, and with good reason, for it is basic to an understanding of the Christian faith. A true understanding of His amazing ministry is only possible by comprehending His unique being.

Is He or is He not God revealed in the flesh? I propose that the consistent and unambiguous witness of the New Testament is that He was fully God and fully man, and yet remained a single personality.

Most errors come about due to a defective view of the person of Christ, and this in turn leads to an inadequate or erroneous view of the nature of His work. The purpose of these studies of His life and work is to present what the Bible has to say about His person, and then to interpret those statements in the context of His actions and words.

It is told of Leonardo da Vinci that, when he was about to depict the face of Christ in his fresco of *The Last Supper,* he prepared himself by prayer and meditation. Yet when he raised his brush to give expression to his devout thoughts, his hand trembled. Such an attitude and reaction is proper for any attempt to set forth the perfections and sufferings of the Son of God, whose work is the unveiling of His person, and whose person makes His work divinely effective.

This volume does not strive to be a theological presentation but rather a devotional and doctrinal treatment of the great facts of the person and work of Christ, in a form suited to the average reader untrained in theology. It is my prayer that the Holy Spirit, who delights to reveal the things of Christ to us, will unveil His glory to those who read this book.

J. OSWALD SANDERS

EDITOR'S NOTE

M y purpose in revising and updating this important work of J. Oswald
Sanders is to make it more accessible for today's reader, especially
in terms of rendering a more devotional tone than the author originally
intended. Even though the book was originally written only fifty years
ago, Sanders still wrote in an older, more archaic style.

I have also condensed the book from thirty-six to thirty-one chapters. Again, with his devotional purpose in mind, I have allowed for daily
readings concerning the life and work of Christ over a given month,
should the reader so choose.

When Sanders wrote *The Incomparable Christ* he was working from
the texts of the King James Version and the *Revised Standard Version*. I have
changed King James Version readings to the *New International Version* in
most instances, but not all. Where Sanders used the *Revised Standard Version* I have retained those readings.

May God the Father bring you into a deeper relationship with Jesus
Christ through His Holy Spirit as you meditate on His life and works.

JAMES S. BELL JR.

1

THE MORAL PERFECTION
OF CHRIST

In a letter published after his death, the poet Robert Browning cited several statements of men of learning concerning the Christian faith, and among them was this one from Charles Lamb: "In trying to predict with some friends as to how they would react if some of the great persons of past ages were to appear suddenly in the flesh once more, one of the friends said, 'And if Christ entered this room?' Lamb changed his attitude at once and said, 'You see if Shakespeare entered we should all rise; if HE appeared, we must kneel.'" This was his view of the glory of Christ.

A similar conclusion was drawn by a brilliant Brahmin (Hindu) scholar. Disturbed by the progress of the Christian faith among his own people, he determined to do all in his power to arrest it. His plan was to prepare a book for widespread distribution highlighting the weaknesses and failings of Christ and exposing the fallacy of believing in Him.

For eleven years he diligently studied the New Testament, searching for inconsistencies in Christ's character and teaching. Not only did he fail to discover any, but he became convinced that the One he sought to discredit was what He claimed to be—the Son of God. The scholar boldly confessed his faith in Christ.

The moral perfection of Christ impresses itself on the serious reader of the Gospels. The evangelists present the portrait of a real man who displays perfection at every stage of His development and in every circumstance of His life. This is all the more remarkable as He did not lock Himself in some secluded cloister but mixed freely and naturally with the imperfect men of His own generation. He became so deeply involved in the life of the ordinary people that His tendency to mix with sinners drew the most bitter criticism of the sanctimonious Pharisees.

And yet there was a perception that He was so ordinary that many of His contemporaries saw Him only as "the carpenter's son," a lowly Nazarene. With eyes blinded by sin and selfishness, they saw no beauty in Him that they should desire Him (Isaiah 53:2). To all except those whose eyes were enlightened by love and faith, His moral grandeur and divine glory passed unnoticed. The ignorant crowds were deceived by the entire absence of pride and self-seeking in Jesus.

PERFECT BLENDING OF CHARACTER

The character of our Lord was wonderfully balanced, with no excessive or deficient qualities. His excellence is recognized not only by Christians but also by Jews and those of other religions. It stands out as faultless and perfect, so even and proportioned that its strength and greatness are not immediately obvious to the casual observer. It has been said that in Jesus' character no strong points were obvious because there were no weaknesses. Strong points necessarily presuppose weakness, but no weaknesses can be found in Him. In the best of men there are obvious inconsistencies, and since the tallest bodies cast the longest shadows, the greater the man, the more glaring his faults are likely to be. With Christ it was quite the contrary. He was without flaw or contradiction.

Virtue degenerates into vice in different ways. Courage may degenerate into cowardice on the one hand or rashness on the other. Purity may slip into either prudery or impurity. The pathway to virtue is narrow and slippery, but in our Lord there was no straying off the path. Throughout His earthly life He maintained every virtue without stain.

His perfect balance of character was displayed in speech as in silence. He never spoke when it would have been wiser to remain silent, never kept silence when He should have spoken. Mercy and judgment blended in all His actions and judgments, yet neither prevailed at the expense of the other. Exact truth and infinite love adorned each other in His winsome personality, for He always spoke the truth in love. His severe denunciations of apostate Jerusalem coincided with His tears (Matthew 23:37). True to His own counsel, He manifested the wisdom of the serpent and the simplicity of the dove. His tremendous inner strength never degenerated into mere self-will. He mastered the difficult art of displaying sympathy without surrendering principle.

The best qualities of both sexes combined in Him. But while possessing all the gentler graces of the female, He could never be regarded as effeminate. Indeed, He was linked in popular thought with the rugged Elijah and the austere John the Baptist (Matthew 16:14). There is contrast yet no contradiction in His delicacy and gentleness in handling people who merited such treatment, and the blistering denunciations He poured on the hypocrites.

Another distinctive feature is that our Lord's character was complete in itself. He entered on life with anything but a passionless simplicity of nature; yet it was a complete and finished character, with entire moral maturity. Most men are notable for one conspicuous virtue or grace—Moses for meekness, Job for patience, John for love. But in Jesus you find *everything*. He is always consistent in Himself. No act or word contradicts anything that has preceded it. The character of Christ is one and the same throughout. He makes no improvements, has no excessive behavior and no eccentricities. His balance is never disturbed or adjusted.

UNIQUENESS OF CHARACTER

The uniqueness of Christ is demonstrated most clearly in the things that every other great human teacher has done, but that He did not do.

No word He spoke needed to be modified or withdrawn, because He never spoke unadvisedly or fell into the sin of exaggeration. No half-truth or misstatement ever crossed His lips. He who was the Truth spoke the whole truth, and no occasion arose for modifying or retracting a single spoken word.

He never apologized for any word or action. And yet, is it not true that the ability to apologize is one of the elements of true greatness? It is the small-minded man who will not stoop to apologize. But Christ performed no action and spoke no word that required apology.

He confessed no sin. The holiest men of all ages have been the most forthright in their confession of shortcoming and failure. Read for example the classic diary of Andrew A. Bonar, the Scottish preacher. But no admission of failure to live up to the highest divine standards came from Jesus' lips. On the contrary, He invited the closest investigation and scrutiny of His life by friend or foe. "Can any of you prove me guilty of sin?" He challenged (John 8:46). His life was an open book. Nothing He did was done in secret. He shouted His criticisms from the housetops. No one else could have survived the withering criticism of His enemies, yet He emerged with His reputation untarnished.

Because that was the case, *He never asked for pardon.* Nowhere is it indicated that He ever felt remorse for sin or exhibited any fear of future punishment. He admonished His disciples when they prayed to say, "Forgive us our debts," but He never related those words to Himself, because He owed no debts, either moral or spiritual.

He never sought advice from even the wisest men of His day. All other great leaders consulted learned men, even Moses and Solomon. On the rare occasions on which well-meaning friends gave advice to Jesus, He rejected it, as for example when His mother reminded Him of the lack of wine at the wedding feast (John 2:4–5).

He never sought to justify unclear conduct, as, for example, when He lay sleeping in the stern of the boat in the midst of a raging storm, apparently indifferent to the fears of His companions. Jesus volunteered no explanation and offered no apology (Mark 4:37–41). His delay in responding to the urgent appeal of the two sisters when Lazarus was ill was equally open to misunderstanding. We would have been unable to refrain from explaining and justifying our seeming lack of concern, but He was content to leave the passage of time and the unfolding of His

Father's plan to vindicate His mysterious actions, as in the story of the raising of Lazarus (John 11).

Finally, *He never asked or permitted prayer for Himself.* True, He invited His three intimate friends to watch with Him but not to pray for Him. Their prayer was to be for themselves lest they enter into temptation (Matthew 26:36–46).

COMBINATION OF CHARACTERISTICS

There have been other people who have lived two lives, one open to the scrutiny of all, the other hidden from most people. In His one person, Jesus possessed two natures that were manifested and exhibited at the same time. Certain qualities that seldom coexist in the same person combined without any contradiction in Him.

An unusual mixture of dependence and independence was observable in the life of the Master. Although conscious that He had at His disposal every human and divine resource, He desired the comfort of human company and sympathy. He exhibited a strong independence from the praise or censure of the crowd, yet the companionship of His inner circle of friends was warmly appreciated.

Joyfulness and seriousness blended in Him perfectly and naturally. The tender words of His farewell discourse are shot through with Christ's particular joy: "I have told you this so that my joy may be in you and that your joy may be complete" (John 15:11). He was "a man of sorrows, and familiar with suffering" (Isaiah 53:3), yet the Scriptures say of Him: "God, your God, has set you above your companions by anointing you with the oil of joy" (Hebrews 1:9).

Although there is no record of our Lord laughing, He leaves the very opposite impression of gloom or legalism. Did He ever actually laugh? Surely if He was anointed by God with the oil of gladness above His contemporaries, there must have been room for holy laughter. It is unthinkable that He constantly paraded His sorrows, poignant though they were. The Gospels unite to present a man winsome, radiant, and irresistibly attractive.

Perhaps the most arresting of these combinations of qualities were those of His majesty and humility. He was a man who was always meek and lowly: "For who is greater, the one who is at the table or the one who serves? Is it not the one who is at the table? But I am among you as one who serves" (Luke 22:27). On occasion His divine majesty blazed through the veil of His humanity. When He was arrested, He said to the soldiers, "I AM," and "they drew back and fell to the ground" (John 18:6). The demonstration of both qualities is seen on the occasion of the foot washing of His disciples. The utter humility of Christ is highlighted by the fact that it was in the full consciousness that "the Father had put all things under his power, and that he had come from God and was returning to God," that He took a towel and washed His followers' dirty feet (John 13:3–5).

The wonder of the unity and uniqueness of His character is the more amazing since He had so short a time in which to work out the seeming contradictions of His soul. He was surely Lord of Himself and of all else besides.

To sum up, "He is altogether lovely." Every element of moral and spiritual beauty resides in Him. In a painting by Michelangelo, Christ is depicted sitting with other men, but the artist has been careful to ensure that the light most strongly falls on His face. The same impression is conveyed in the word pictures of the four Gospels. In the succeeding chapters it will be my task to examine the glorious colors that emanate from the prism of His holy person and redemptive work.

KEY INSIGHT
INTO THE LIFE AND WORK OF CHRIST

In His character,
Christ had a perfect
balance and blending
of all the virtues,
each to perfection.

2

THE PREEXISTENCE
OF CHRIST

I AM what I was—God.
I was not what I am—Man.
I am now called both—
GOD and MAN.

This old Latin inscription, chiseled in marble, simply explains the consistent teaching of the Scriptures concerning the origin and incarnation of our Lord. While affirming His real humanity, this concise theological statement carefully safeguards the no less vital fact of His preexistence and Godhead. It will be noted that Christ's existence prior to His conception and birth is nowhere in Scripture argued as a doctrine but is everywhere assumed and used as the basis of the doctrines of the incarnation and atonement. His birth in Bethlehem was not His origin, only His incarnation as a human being.

Indeed, how could there be an incarnation without a previous existence? To deny the latter renders the former impossible. To go back further, could there be a Trinity were there no preexistent Son of God? The one necessarily presupposes the other. Christ's preexistence is not a matter of purely academic interest; it is the foundation on which the whole superstructure of the Christian faith rests. If He was not preexistent,

He cannot be God, and if He is not God, He cannot be Creator and Redeemer.

Jesus was unique among men in that His birth did not mark His origin but only His appearance as a man on the stage of human existence. This is true of no other human being. Jesus was the meeting place of eternity and time, the blending of deity and humanity, the junction of heaven and earth. His origin was not related to His birth, nor was His nature dependent only on human ancestry. His nature was derived from His eternal being. He did not *become* God's Son at the Incarnation or when He rose from the dead. He is God, supreme and without beginning.

Our Lord was conscious of a previous existence. He spoke of the glory He had with the Father before the world existed (John 17:5). He claimed preexistence in explicit and unmistakable terms: "I came from God. I came from the Father and entered the world" (John 16:27–28). Every other person entered life as the natural climax of biological processes and as a new creature, but Jesus knew neither beginning of days nor end of life (Hebrews 7:3).

CHRIST IN HIS PREEXISTENT STATE

Since our Lord nowhere attempts to give a systematic teaching concerning Himself, what can we know of Him in His preexistent state? A careful study of the Scriptures reveals a surprising wealth of assumptions as well as explicit statements regarding His earlier existence.

The Old Testament is not without mention of His preexistence. In the same verse in which Micah foretold the scene of the Incarnation, the prophet asserted of the Messiah that His "origins are from of old, from ancient times" (Micah 5:2). He was not only a man of earthly origin but of a heavenly nature as well.

Jesus described Himself to Nicodemus as "the one who came from heaven" (John 3:13). He often spoke out of the awareness of His own preexistence. "You loved me before the creation of the world" (John 17:24).

When Pilate asked Jesus, "Where do you come from?" He remained silent but left no doubt of His earlier existence (John 19:9–11). When the cynical Pharisees threw out the challenge "You are not yet fifty years old, and you have seen Abraham!" Jesus gave the equally challenging reply "Before Abraham was born, I am!" (John 8:57–58). Those words, which contrasted Abraham's entrance into existence and His own timeless being, are a clear assertion of preexistence. They also imply a claim of unity with the Jehovah of the Old Testament.

In His moving High Priestly Prayer, Jesus spoke of His yearning for a resumption of the glorious relationship that had eternally existed between Himself and His Father, only interrupted by His incarnation: "Glorify me in your presence with the glory I had with you before the world began" (John 17:5). This is not just a dreamed-of preexistence but an actual and conscious awareness of His existence at the Father's side. This yearning for the Father throws light on His frequent withdrawals into a mountain solitude where He could recapture something of the atmosphere of His heavenly home.

An illuminating glimpse of the relationship of the eternal Father and the eternal Son is suggested in Proverbs. "The LORD brought me forth as the first of his works, before his deeds of old; I was appointed from eternity, from the beginning, before the world began. . . . I was there when he set the heavens in place, . . . when he marked out the foundations of the earth. Then I was the craftsman at his side. I was filled with delight day after day, rejoicing always in his presence" (Proverbs 8:22–23, 27, 29–30). It would appear that here "wisdom" is more than the personification of an attribute of God but is rather a foreshadowing of Christ Himself, who is the wisdom of God.

"Wisdom" is personified in much the same way as is "the Word" (John 1:1). There are striking correspondences between the personified divine wisdom in Proverbs and the incarnate divine Word in John. In his prologue, John asserts that all that Wisdom declares of herself was true of the Word who "became flesh and made his dwelling among us" (John 1:14) and who "was God" and "was with God in the beginning" (John 1:1–2).

CHRIST'S RICHES IN ETERNITY

Paul links Christ's precedence in time with His preeminence as Creator and Preserver. "He is before all things, and in him all things hold together" (Colossians 1:17). He compresses into three pregnant words the condition of our Lord in His former state of glory: "He was rich" (2 Corinthians 8:9). This shows the magnitude of the love that caused Him to lay aside what one writer has described as "the splendours and prerogatives of deity, the exercise of infinite power and the disclosures of supreme majesty."

"His love transcends all human measure," exclaimed P. T. Forsyth, "if only, out of love, He renounced the glory of heavenly being for all He here became. Only then could we grasp the full stay and comfort of words like these. 'Who shall separate us from the love of Christ?' Unlike us, He *chose* the oblivion of birth and the humiliation of life. He consented not only to die, but to be born. . . . What He gave up was the fulness, power and immunity of a heavenly life."

He was certainly not rich in the sense in which we use the word. Then in what did these riches that He renounced for our enrichment consist? Divine riches cannot be weighed by earth's scales. They were, of course, spiritual, not material. And are not all true riches spiritual?

Among others, the following three demonstrate His riches found in His heavenly home:

He was rich in the love of the home. "My Father's house" (John 14:2) was a phrase that conjured up nostalgic memories of past joys and loving fellowship. In His High Priestly Prayer He said to His Father, "You loved me before the creation of the world" (John 17:24). Not luxurious furnishings or priceless works of art but mutual understanding and reciprocal love are the true riches found in the home. In His Father's house, those had been the Son's from eternity, and, in addition, He had the love and adoration of all the heavenly host of angels. He was rich in home love.

He was rich in harmony of the home. The unity of the Godhead was unmarred by discord. Father, Son, and Holy Spirit delight to honor one another. "I and the Father are one" (John 10:30), Jesus claimed, implying they were one not only in essence but also in attitude and purpose. The persons of the Trinity cooperated for our redemption in perfect harmony. The Father planned salvation. The Son made the plan possible to be realized by yielding up His life to death on the cross. The Spirit used His fiery energies to implement the plan. It was His appreciation of this harmony that inspired our Lord to pray for His followers: "that they may be one *as we are one*" (John 17:11, italics added). The harmony of His heavenly home was complete and satisfying.

He was rich in resources of the home. Every biblical allusion to the Father's house is one of surpassing beauty and splendor. It seems as though the inspired writers, at a loss to describe its magnificence and fullness, ransacked the universe for conceptions to convey something of the glories that Christ renounced in the Incarnation. "The wall was made of jasper, and the city of pure gold, as pure as glass. The foundations of the city walls were decorated with every kind of precious stone. . . . The twelve gates were twelve pearls . . . [and the] street of the city was of pure gold, like transparent glass" (Revelation 21:18–19, 21).

In His Father's house, every created being was at His immediate command. "Do you think I cannot call on my Father, and he will at once put at my disposal more than twelve legions of angels?" (Matthew 26:53) was Jesus' challenge to His enemies. He could have anything He desired, and it was His desire that His disciples should share in His Father's bounty. "My Father will give you whatever you ask in my name" (John 16:23).

CHRIST IN OLD TESTAMENT TIMES

Our Lord's first appearance on earth was not when He was born of His virgin mother. Of these mysterious earlier appearances, or "theophanies," Scripture simply records the fact without offering any explanation. Theophanies differ in nature from visions. It is recorded, for example, that God appeared as a man to Jacob and wrestled with him. Speaking of his experience, Jacob said, "I saw God face to face, and yet my life was spared" (Genesis 32:30). In Jacob's experience, as in other theophanies, it is generally accepted that it was the second person of the Trinity who appeared in human form, since "no one has ever seen God, but God the One and Only, who is at the Father's side, has made him known" (John 1:18). It is He who appeared to Joshua (Joshua 5:13–15) and to the three young men in the fiery furnace (Daniel 3:25).

It appears that in Old Testament times God came in the *form* of a man, whereas in the Incarnation He actually *became* man. In both Testaments it is the same person of the Godhead, the eternal Son, through whom the invisible God appeared to man. In the theophanies God took human form only temporarily and for a limited purpose. But when Christ was born, He assumed our humanity forever. Today He is still "the man Christ Jesus" (1 Timothy 2:5).

It will be noted that many of these manifestations of Christ were in angelic form. "The Angel of Jehovah" is the usual title. In many cases the angelic visitor was at first mistaken for a man.

Christ could have come in angelic form, but then sinning men could not have been redeemed. Angels cannot die, and sinners are human. No angel would have been competent to act as substitute for the sinner (Hebrews 2:14–18).

KEY INSIGHT
INTO THE LIFE AND WORK OF CHRIST

Christ existed eternally with the Father before becoming born as a man on this earth.

3

THE INCARNATION
OF CHRIST

M an has always craved a God who is tangible and visible. As he bows
to stones and trees, the idolater is mutely expressing the desire of
the human heart for a god who can be seen. Job lamented that although
he sought for God, he could not see Him. "If I go to the east, he is not
there; if I go to the west, I do not find him. . . . I do not see him" (Job
23:8–9). Philip shared the same longing when he asked, "Lord, show us
the Father and that will be enough for us" (John 14:8).

God's answer to this universal longing, the incarnation of His Son,
was implied in Jesus' answer to Philip, "Anyone who has seen me has
seen the Father" (John 14:9). The clear implication is that in the acts and
attitudes of the Son we have a revelation of the attitudes and activities of
the Father. "No one has ever seen God, but God the One and Only, who
is at the Father's side, has made him known" (John 1:18; cf. KJV).

THE MYSTERY OF HIS BIRTH

The mystery of the Incarnation will never be fully explained until
"we know even as we are known." But it is not the only enigma in this
mysterious world, and as Lecerf said, "The presence of mystery is the foot-
print of the divine." We are daily surrounded by mysterious facts, which

are facts nevertheless. We may not understand how Jesus could be at the same time fully divine and yet really human, but that need be no permanent obstacle to faith. These facts have been believed by many of the greatest minds of the ages.

When we remember that it required four millennia for God to prepare the world for the advent of His Son, the stupendous importance He attached to that event becomes clear. Is it likely that such an event, unique in eternity as in time, would occur in the ordinary course of nature? The astounding fact is that with all its magnificent system of communications, the great Roman world remained in absolute unconsciousness of the presence of God. The entrance of the Creator into the world was so hidden as to warrant no notice.

If, as science requires, every event must have an adequate cause, then the presence of a sinless man in the midst of universally sinful people implies a miracle. The *how* of His birth becomes believable when the *who* of the birth is taken into account. Only in isolation from the unique person of Christ does the virgin birth create difficulties. The preexistence of Christ would necessitate a miracle of birth.

An orthodox Jew once asked a Jewish Christian, "Suppose a son were born among us today, and it was said that he was born of a virgin, would you believe it?"

"Yes," was the reply, "I would believe it if he were such a son!"

Anselm reviewed four ways in which God can make man:

1. By the law of natural generation—a man and a woman.
2. Without the agency of either man or woman—as Adam.
3. A man without a woman—as Eve.
4. Through the divine empowering of a man and a woman both past age—as Abraham and Sarah.

If these are admitted, as they must be if the Scripture records are accepted as authoritative and trustworthy, it is but a step to believe that

5. Jesus was born of a woman without a man; He was begotten of the Holy Spirit (Matthew 1:20; Luke 1:35).

If we accept that Jesus was the incarnate Son of God, does not belief in the Virgin Birth become logically inevitable? Who could be the Father of the Son of God but God Himself?

This doctrine was accepted by the early church and is included in all the great Christian creeds. Justin Martyr included it among the main items of Christian belief, the apologist Aristides accepted it, and Ignatius insisted on it—and those three lived very close to the apostolic age and to the documents setting forth the Virgin Birth.

THE MEANING OF VIRGIN BIRTH

What does the term mean? It does not imply that Jesus was born in a manner different from other children. He was born in exactly the same way as any other baby. Nor does it suggest that there was merely a miraculous *conception,* as in the case of Elizabeth, who was past age when John the Baptist was conceived in her womb. It does not mean *immaculate conception* as taught by the Roman Catholic church, for that dogma asserts that Mary was conceived and born without original sin, a claim for which there is not a shred of scriptural support. Rather, the conception of Christ was a conception of a virgin entirely without parallel. Contrary to the course of nature, Jesus was *miraculously conceived* in the womb of Mary. In His case, the ordinary processes of the transmission of human characteristics were interrupted by the miraculous conception.

Such a birth was foreshadowed in the Old Testament. The earliest Bible prophecy enshrines and implies this unique event. "I will put enmity between thee and the woman, and between thy seed and her seed; it shall bruise thy head, and thou shalt bruise his heel" (Genesis 3:15 KJV). Only here are the words *her seed* used. Elsewhere it is uniformly the seed of the man. This is a unique conception in human history.

The sign divinely given to Ahaz was that "the virgin will be with child and will give birth to a son, and will call him Immanuel" (Isaiah 7:14). Words could hardly be more explicit, and Matthew saw their fulfillment in the manner of our Lord's birth. The word for "virgin" used here, *almah,* has given rise to considerable controversy, and it is maintained by opponents of the supernatural that the word means simply a young woman of marriageable age, not necessarily a virgin, for which *bethulah* is the term used. It is unfortunate for this view that *bethulah* is used of a bride weeping for her husband, while *almah* is used in this and six other places, but never in any other sense than an unmarried maiden.

Martin Luther threw out a challenge on this point: "If a Jew or a Christian can prove to me that in any other passage of Scripture *almah* means a married woman, I will give him a hundred florins, although God alone knows where I may find them."

ALTERNATIVES TO VIRGIN BIRTH

It is conceded that the Bible does not demand belief in the Virgin Birth as a prerequisite for salvation, but it does indicate that the *fact* of the Virgin Birth must be true if we are to be saved. It is possible for a man to be saved without knowing details of the process, just as babies are born without any knowledge of embryology. It is the *integrity* of the fact, not our *knowledge* of it that lays the basis for our salvation.

At the close of one of his services, the late Harry Emerson Fosdick said, "I want to assure you that I do not believe in the virgin birth of Christ, and I hope none of you do." He was doubtless sincere, but can such an attitude be justified? It is the element of miracle that proves a stumbling block to such men. But if Joseph and Mary, who were sinners by nature and deed, could have given birth to a sinless man such as Jesus, would not an even greater miracle be involved?

Let us consider the alternatives that face us if this doctrine is fiction and not fact.

1. The New Testament narratives are proved false, and the book is robbed of its authority on other matters also.
2. Mary, instead of being blessed among women, is branded as unchaste, for Joseph asserted that Jesus was not his son.
3. Jesus becomes the natural child of sinful parents, which at once rules out His preexistence, with the result that there was no real incarnation.

4. We are deprived of any adequate explanation of His unique character and sinless life.
5. If He was begotten of a human father—and that is the only alternative to virgin birth—He was not the second person of the Trinity, as He claimed, and therefore had no power to forgive sin.
6. If this miracle is denied, where do we stop? Logically, we should deny all miracles. The question really is, Are we willing to accept the supernatural claims of Scripture or not?

OBJECTIONS TO VIRGIN BIRTH

Before considering some objections, we should note that this doctrine is at variance with nothing taught elsewhere in the New Testament; but on the other hand, it positively corresponds to the preexistence of Christ and His incarnation.

Some contend that *Jesus' having only one human parent would not of itself guarantee sinlessness.* That may well be true, but it was not the mere biological fact of having only one parent that preserved Him from the taint of hereditary sin. A moral fact cannot be explained merely in terms of physical considerations. Calvin maintained that His conception was holy and untainted, not because man had no part in the conception but because He was sanctified by the Spirit, so that His generation was as pure and holy as it would have been before Adam's Fall. It was by the special agency of the Holy Spirit, who overshadowed Mary (Luke 1:35). It was by the direct activity of God that Jesus was kept from the contamination of Mary's sinful nature.

Others argue that *both genealogies in Matthew and Luke trace His descent through Joseph and not through Mary at all.* This only appears to be the case. Luke's genealogy is that of Mary, who was apparently of the same tribe and family as Joseph. Matthew records the genealogy of Joseph, because it was necessary that the Messiah's right to the throne of David should be established. It is true that Jesus was a lineal descendant of David through His mother, but as a woman had no right to the throne, her son would be similarly disqualified. But as the legally adopted son of

Joseph, who was also of the Davidic line, Jesus had a legal claim to the throne. From the two genealogies it is established that Jesus was of the seed of David by natural as well as legal descent.

In this connection an interesting suggestion has been advanced: "Probably the Matthan of Matthew is the Matthat of Luke, and Jacob and Heli were brothers; and Heli's son Joseph and Jacob's daughter Mary first cousins. Joseph, as male heir to his uncle Jacob, who had only one child, Mary, would marry her according to Numbers 36:8. Thus the genealogy of the inheritance (Matthew's) and that of natural descent (Luke's) would be primarily Joseph's, then Mary's also."

The writers who included these tables in their records were the men who recorded the Virgin Birth. Obviously they were conscious of no contradiction between their narratives and the genealogies. Each was careful to guard against saying that Joseph was the father of Jesus. "Jacob the father of Joseph, the husband of Mary, of whom [feminine pronoun] was born Jesus" (Matthew 1:16). "Jesus . . . was the son, so it was thought, of Joseph" (Luke 3:23).

THE ARGUMENT FROM SILENCE

The peril of pressing the argument from silence too far is illustrated in the old claim of the criminal who maintained that only two men saw him steal, whereas he could bring a hundred who did not, and therefore he should be acquitted!

Because certain New Testament writers—Mark, John, and Paul—do not clearly refer to the event, it is asserted that their silence argues against its truth. It is dangerous to argue from silence to ignorance, for the one does not necessarily imply the other. Actually, the argument proves too much. Mark is equally silent on the whole subject of our Lord's birth. Must we therefore conclude that He was not born at all? His gospel begins with the public ministry of Jesus. Then, too, Mark refers to Jesus not as the carpenter's son but as the Son of Mary.

And what of John? If no such miracle as the Virgin Birth occurred, how are we to understand this statement: "The Word became flesh and made his dwelling among us" (John 1:14)? Is that not more than a hint of the Incarnation?

In the words of John 1:13 scholars of widely differing schools find a distinct reference to the subject. On this point Samuel Zwemer writes: "Here those who believe the Word are those 'who were begotten, not of blood, nor of the will of the flesh, nor of the will of man, but of God.' But according to the testimony of Tertullian there was an early second-century reading of this text which had the singular instead of the plural. It would then read, 'He was begotten not of blood, nor of the will of the flesh, nor of the will of man, but of God.'"

In his *de Carne Christi* Tertullian wrote: "I shall make more use of this passage after I have confronted those who have tampered with it. They maintain it was written in the plural, as if designating those who were before mentioned as believing on His name. But how can this be when all who believe . . . are by virtue of the common principle of the human race born of blood and of the will of the flesh and of the will of man?—as indeed is Valentinus himself. The expression is in the singular, as referring to the Lord. He was born of God. . . . As flesh, however, He is not of blood, nor of the will of the flesh, nor of man, because it was by the will of God that the word was made flesh."

If this old reading is correct, John denies any human paternity to Christ and asserts the Virgin Birth in the clearest possible way. St. Augustine in his *Confessions* quotes this same verse from John's gospel in the singular and takes it to refer to the Virgin Birth. "Also I found there that God the Word was born not of blood, nor of the will of a husband, nor the will of the flesh, but of God."

There is a tradition that on one occasion John left the public baths at Ephesus when Cerinthus, the Gnostic heretic, entered. John's profound aversion to Cerinthus stemmed from the fact that he taught that Jesus was the natural son of Joseph and Mary. Could not John's aversion indicate a knowledge of the Virgin Birth?

In any case, John could not be ignorant of the doctrine, for he had access to the Synoptic Gospels, and Mary lived with him after the

Crucifixion. Had he known that the tradition was without foundation, it is incredible that he would have made no reference to that fact.

Although Paul makes no direct reference to the doctrine, if he is silent about the Virgin Birth, he is equally silent about the human paternity of Jesus. Yet he invariably employed some unusual and significant expressions when referring to the Incarnation.

This is especially the case in Galatians 4. In this chapter Paul used the word "born" several times, but in speaking of Christ's birth he used a different Greek word from the one he employed when he spoke of the births of Ishmael and Isaac. Galatians 4:4 reads, "But when the time had fully come, God sent his Son, born of a woman, born under the law." Here the Greek word translated "born" has the meaning of "cause to be" or "to become." This concept is somewhat captured in the King James reading: "When the fulness of the time was come, God sent forth his Son, *made* of a woman, *made* under the law" (italics added). In Galatians 4:23 and 29 the Greek term Paul used for the births of Ishmael and Isaac was the Greek term ordinarily used to refer to birth. Nothing Paul wrote in any way casts doubt upon this important tenet of the evangelical faith, but rather he assumed it in his writings.

KEY INSIGHT
INTO THE LIFE AND WORK OF CHRIST

Jesus Christ is both fully divine and fully human, and this could only be achieved by a miraculous conception in the womb of Mary.

4

THE CHILDHOOD
OF CHRIST

A nd the child grew and became strong; he was filled with wisdom, and the grace of God was upon him" (Luke 2:40). This is all we know about the childhood of Jesus, but the silences of God are as significant as His speech. It does not satisfy our curiosity, but there is sufficient information revealed to assure us of His real humanity and full identity with the human race. Although He began life as a *perfect* child, we must not forget that He began it as a perfect *child*. He did not burst upon the world as a mature adult but as a tiny infant—in striking contrast to the Greek gods, who descended to earth fully grown and well armed. In His incarnation Jesus submitted Himself to the sinless limitations of growth and development inherent in membership of the human race. The Gospels do not undertake to provide us with a biography of Jesus of Nazareth but with a history of Jesus the Savior.

APOCRYPHAL LEGENDS

In the light of the pseudogospels of the early centuries, which were full of silly fables, the silence of the evangelists concerning incidents in the Christ child's boyhood are the more significant. There are no stories of a precocious child. Some of the apocryphal gospels are still in existence, two of them entitled "the Gospel of Infancy." "These were written by Christians; by men who wished to honor Christ in all they said about him," writes W. Hanna. "And yet we find them narrating that when boys interrupted Jesus in His play or ran against Him in the village street, He looked on them and denounced them, and they fell down and died."

Such blasphemous absurdities are a travesty of the truth, as though the Son of God would descend to pathetic displays of divine power and even acts of petty vengeance. Here is a warning not to intrude when God has not spoken. The reason no amazing and extraordinary experiences are recorded is that apparently none happened. The silence of the inspired writers tacitly assures us that His growth and development were those of a normal child, not of a precocious prodigy. He experienced normal progress, although the absence of sin would undoubtedly enable more rapid intellectual and moral growth and development. He grew in body. He waxed strong in spirit. He increased in the wisdom of mind and heart.

THE NAZARETH HOME

Jesus' home of Nazareth (Luke 2:4, 39) was a small, despised village in the Galilee region, inhabited by unsophisticated people. An indication of its reputation among the Jews is implicit in Nathanael's question, "Nazareth! Can anything good come from there?" (John 1:46; see also 7:41, 52). That such a village should be chosen by God as a home for His Son is another significant element in the divine emptying process.

His family comprised at least eight members, and maybe more. "Isn't this the carpenter's son? Isn't his mother's name Mary, and aren't his brothers James, Joseph, Simon and Judas? Aren't all his sisters with us?" (Matthew 13:55–56) was the question of his fellow citizens. So in that cramped Eastern home, the Lord of glory experienced the disciplines of life found in a larger family, living at close quarters with sinful brothers and sisters, yet He emerged from the experience "without sin." His reference to a prophet not being without honor except in His own house (Matthew 13:57) probably reflected the loneliness of His sinless childhood.

The influence, example, and teaching of His mother doubtless played an important part in His development. Everything indicates that she was one of those rare women whose glory it is to live a noble life, losing themselves in it, and desiring to be glorified only in its usefulness. Mary's song reveals her as a devout, high-minded woman, fervently patriotic and a student of Scripture. Her song is patterned on that of an older saintly woman of the Old Testament, Hannah.

HIS NATURAL DEVELOPMENT

In order to be "made like his brothers" (Hebrews 2:17), our Lord subjected Himself to the common laws of human infancy and childhood.

He experienced normal physical development. "The child grew and became strong." Pictures of the child Jesus with a halo do Him a great disservice. He was indistinguishable from other children, except for the absence of sin. He passed through all the stages of a natural development, delighting to scramble up the hills around His home.

Jesus grew at the same rate as other boys, and His amazing physical endurance in the succeeding years bore eloquent evidence of physical foundations well laid during youth. From the ease and accuracy with which He made use of the happenings of everyday life in His teaching, it is obvious that He was an observant child. Like the other children of the village, since there were no parks, He doubtless played in the marketplace (Luke 7:31–32) and joined in their bodybuilding games. He was neither ascetic nor Stoic.

To fulfill the psalmist's prophecy "Thou art fairer than the children of men" (Psalm 45:2 KJV), He must have been an unusually attractive child physically. His voice must have held early promise of the rich and vibrant tones that later thrilled and held the multitudes spellbound and caused the temple guards sent to arrest Him to exclaim, "No one ever spoke the way this man does" (John 7:46).

He advanced in mental capacity. "Jesus grew in wisdom" (Luke 2:52 NIV). He was not an adult infant. He acquired the power of speech as did other children. He gradually gained familiarity with the ordinary branches of human knowledge. He learned to read (Luke 4:17) and write

(John 8:6–8). His knowledge came to Him by degrees, but every degree of growth was perfect.

So body and mind developed together, and He displayed manly vigor and mental power. It is impossible to penetrate the mystery of His gradual development, but Scripture asserts it as a fact.

HIS EDUCATION

Although the Gospels shed no light on the education of Jesus, it is possible to gain some knowledge from the customs of the day. His first instruction would be at the knee of His mother. She would teach Him to chant psalms and would instruct Him in the basics of the Hebrew law and history. From the preparations for the Passover festival, He would be told the story of redemption in the Old Testament.

In a Jewish village the size of Nazareth there would be a school, known as "The House of the Book," to which Jesus would be sent at the age of six. The rulers of the synagogue were the teachers. Up to the age of ten, the Old Testament Scriptures were the only textbook. For five years the children memorized the Old Testament (Deuteronomy 6:7), especially the Pentateuch, until "the Jew knew the Law better than his own name." From His familiarity with the Scriptures, it might be inferred that there was a copy of the sacred scrolls in the home.

The first book to be studied was Leviticus. What were the thoughts that jostled in the mind of the eager young scholar as He read the ritual of sacrifice that foreshadowed the sacrifice of God's Lamb? James Stalker remarks that no stain of sin clouded His vision of divine things, and His soul would have inklings, growing to convictions, that He was the One in whom their predictions were destined to be realized.

At the age of twelve the scholar became a "son of the Law" and was robed in the garments of a man. From here on he was regarded as a free moral agent, responsible for his own actions. The initiatory rite might be compared to our joining the church, or confirmation. This was probably in view when Jesus made His first journey to Jerusalem.

What languages did He speak? He certainly knew Aramaic. When the Jews returned from the captivity, they spoke Aramaic, the language spoken by the Persian masters. His quotations indicate that He read in the original Hebrew and not in a Greek translation.

"On the Sabbath day he went into the synagogue, as was his custom. And he stood up to read" (Luke 4:16). His talks were full of quotations from the Old Testament. Then, too, His native Galilee was full of Greek-speaking inhabitants. By reason of its position, Galilee was exposed to inescapable Greek influences. It was probably in Greek that He communicated with the people of Tyre and Sidon. It is quite likely that He was master of Hebrew, Aramaic, and Greek.

Although denied a university education, for He did not, like Paul, sit at the feet of a Gamaliel, in His later ministry Jesus displayed such a mastery of all branches of education that the rabbis exclaimed in amazement: "How did this man get such learning without having studied?" (John 7:15). Much of His spare time would be spent in the synagogue at Nazareth where He was one of the expositors of the Scriptures.

Horace Bushnell wrote very fondly of the child Jesus, "In His childhood everyone loved Him. He is shown growing up in favor with God and man, a child so lovely and beautiful that heaven and earth appear to smile on him together. So when it is added that the child grew and waxed strong in spirit, filled with wisdom, and more than all, that the grace or beautifying power of God was upon Him, we look on the unfolding of a sacred flower, and seem to scent a fragrance wafted on us from other worlds."

KEY INSIGHT
INTO THE LIFE AND WORK OF CHRIST

Jesus grew up in humble, ordinary surroundings, and His development was that of a normal child, yet without sin.

5

THE YOUTH
OF CHRIST

"And Jesus grew in wisdom and stature, and in favor with God and men" (Luke 2:52). It is significant that the silence shrouding the first thirty years of our Lord's earthly life is broken only once, and then to record an incident that occurred when He was twelve years of age (Luke 2:42–51). This incident recounted by Luke is the one authentic portion of an otherwise untold story. Why was this single episode selected by the inspiring Spirit from such a wealth of material? Its uniqueness is a measure of its importance, for here alone are we given any insight into the inner probings of His mind as He reached adolescence.

At the age of twelve a Jewish boy crossed the boundary between childhood and youth. Becoming a "son of the Law," He assumed for Himself the religious responsibilities that had previously rested on His parents. Now He must observe the ceremonial law and attend the prescribed annual festivals at Jerusalem. It was when He attained this critical age that Jesus, with His parents and friends, made His first journey to observe the Passover feast in Jerusalem.

THE JERUSALEM JOURNEY

A typical pilgrimage to Jerusalem is graphically reconstructed by W. Robertson Nicoll.

Their road was haunted by wild beasts and banditti. For defence they kept together, and as they journeyed they sang their songs, probably the fifteen psalms after the 119th. They would sing among the Arab tribes, "Woe is me, that I sojourn in Mesech, that I dwell in the tents of Kedar" [Psalm 120:5]. When they escaped the troops of their foes they would sing, "Our soul is escaped as a bird out of the snare of the fowler" [Psalm 124:7]. When they were journeying in cheerful accord, they sang, "Behold, how good and how pleasant it is for brethren to dwell together in unity" [Psalm 133:1].

Jesus would take part in their songs and understand their meaning. . . . When Jerusalem came in sight, and the pilgrims shouted, "I will lift up mine eyes unto the hills, from whence cometh my help" [Psalm 121:1], when the mass of the great temple, white on the uplifted rock, fell on His eyes, what must His feelings have been?

To the village boy the shining spires, the vast throngs of people in His Father's house with busy priests, altars, and ascending incense, must have been an exciting yet sobering experience. Participating in the sacred services of the Passover in these hallowed precincts must have had a solemn effect on Him. Without doubt this visit was an important watershed in His life and brought about a deepening consciousness that between Him and His God there existed a relationship unique among men. He would delight in instruction given by the learned doctors of the Law, who came out from the Sanhedrin and taught the people in the temple courts.

The distressing discovery. The festival was over, and the crowds began the journey home, among them Joseph and Mary, and presumably Jesus. Since it was customary for the youths of the party to travel and sleep together, Joseph and Mary were not concerned at her son's absence from her side. But unconcern gave place to extreme anxiety when at night they failed to find Him among His companions. They had traveled homeward "thinking he was in their company" (Luke 2:44).

Never before had He caused them a moment's anxiety, and such was their confidence in Him that His nonappearance in their party had aroused no concern. It is noteworthy that He must have enjoyed considerable freedom in His boyhood. Many parents would not have allowed their children out of sight!

The distress of Joseph and Mary as the time passed without locating Him is not difficult to imagine. Had some accident happened to Him? Had He fallen ill? Was someone seeking His life (Matthew 2:13, 20)? Had Mary by her negligence failed in her sacred responsibilities? It is in the light of this wholly understandable anxiety that we must interpret the first word of reproof she had ever addressed to Him. The word she used in addressing Him was a tender mother-word, perhaps the equivalent of the Scottish "bairn." "My bairn, why hast thou thus dealt with us?"

The cryptic answer. Probably to His mother's surprise, He did not give the expected explanation or apology. "Why were you searching for me?" was His question back to Mary. "Didn't you know I had to be in my Father's house?" (Luke 2:49). By this He implied that there was less reason for them to be astonished at His remaining behind than for Him to be surprised at their search for Him. The very way in which He set "my Father" against Mary's "your father" indicated the clear conviction that God was uniquely His Father, and He therefore tactfully disowned any human relationship with Joseph. It has been suggested that on His first visit to the temple, Mary may have told Him the secret of His infancy. This would not be inconsistent with His statement on this occasion.

The seven days of the paschal feast had been too short for His eager soul and inquiring mind. Already the zeal of His Father's house was consuming Him (John 2:17). His true home was not the humble home in Nazareth but here amid the worship and ritual of the temple.

Acting in response to the call that had been growing louder in His spirit, He decided to remain behind to learn more from the leading religious teachers of the day. "I *must* be in my Father's house," or "about my Father's business" (Luke 2:49 KJV). It was under family compulsion that He had remained in the temple, and He must obey the call of the Spirit within, even at the risk of being misunderstood by those whom He loved dearly and to whom He had up to then given unquestioning obedience.

As Jesus sat among the doctors of the Law hearing their discourse, there was opportunity for Him to put His questions, for the Jewish mode of learning was mainly based on a catechism, and a great variety of questions was permitted. May it have been during these interchanges that Jesus gained His first knowledge of the traditions of the elders, which He later excoriated?

His wisdom was unusual, His statements were remarkable, His questions were penetrating, and all who heard Him were astonished. This was not precocity, a mind that was advanced beyond the boy's age, but something of a far higher quality, a mind filled with heavenly wisdom, yet unassuming, and only eager to learn. At last He could unburden His heart, and find the answer to the serious problems that had crowded into His mind in Nazareth. If the rabbis thought that they had discovered one of the great rabbis of the future, they were not mistaken.

Joseph and Mary found Him where they should have first sought Him—in His Father's house, engaged in His Father's business. Where would our friends and acquaintances first look for us?

THE SEQUEL TO THE STORY

Jesus had now reached a great crisis. What would be His attitude when He returned to His Nazareth home? In the simple words "He went down to Nazareth with them and was obedient to them" (Luke 2:51), Luke summed up the work of Jesus until His baptism. He developed from boyhood to manhood demonstrating obedience both to His human parents and His divine Father.

The curtain then falls on the boyhood, youth, and early manhood of the Son of Man. It seemed an anticlimax but was in reality a great step forward. Then began eighteen years of hidden discipline and training, during which He was "tempted in every way . . . yet was without sin" (Hebrews 4:15). At home He learned the habit of self-surrender and exact obedience (Hebrews 5:8) that characterized His attitude to His Father and culminated in death on a cross. The Son of Man thus provided a pattern for Christian young people in their relations with their parents.

It is idle to speculate about the time when Jesus first became conscious of the fact that He was God's Son in a unique sense and had a mes-sianic function to fulfill. James Stalker says, "I cannot trust myself even to think of a time when He did not know what His work in this world was to be." Some assert that He possessed this consciousness when a babe on His mother's breast, others that it dawned on Him only when He visited the temple.

But where Scripture is silent, it is wise to refrain from speculation. There are certain things that we do know. We know that He was as di-vine when a dependent baby as when He ascended to the heavenly throne. We know that at the age of twelve He was conscious of being in a unique sense the Son of God. Whether His study of the Scriptures and the witness of the Spirit within had disclosed to Him the mystery of His earthly manifestation, we have no means of knowing and no ne-cessity to know. Suffice it to say that it was early in life that He knew that God was His Father and that He was His Servant and Son.

KEY INSIGHT
INTO THE LIFE AND WORK OF CHRIST

Even at the early age of twelve, Jesus demonstrated a remarkable wisdom and understanding based upon the Scriptures.

6

THE EARTHLY
OCCUPATION OF CHRIST

The life of our Lord has been so idealized by its sacred associations that we are apt to miss some of its most comforting and practical lessons from fear of profaning its sacredness. His earthly occupation is one of these.

We know absolutely nothing of eighteen years of Christ's life except what is contained in the words "the carpenter" (Mark 6:3). This is all that divine wisdom has seen fit to preserve for us. What a title for the Lord of glory!

What is the significance of the fact that, out of all possible occupations, God chose for His Son in His incarnation the lot of a laborer? Why did the only One who could have chosen His earthly vocation without any restriction choose to become a carpenter? It is not difficult to conceive the wonder and consternation of the angelic host to see the great Jehovah, Creator of the rolling spheres, humble Himself to toil with saw and hammer at a carpenter's bench for eighteen years. They would see Him who made the heavens stoop to shape with His own hands a yoke for oxen.

Whatever else this act of humility signified, it meant that Jesus identified Himself fully with the great bulk of mankind, the common people. It gave men's common toil everlasting honor. It acquainted the Master with the feelings of the common people and gave Him insight into man's inmost thoughts. His willingness to occupy so lowly a sphere for so long a time affords us both example and incentive to be willing to do our common tasks joyously.

In common with all other Jewish boys, Jesus was required to learn a trade. What more natural than that He should be apprenticed to His foster father and become the village carpenter? In this connection it will be remembered that in keeping with the custom of the times, Paul mastered the intricacies of the tentmaker's art as well as his university studies.

It is a challenging thought, and one that should be closely observed by those who are preparing for a life of service for God, that our divine Lord spent six times as long working at the carpenter's bench as He did in His world-shaking ministry. He did not cut short the hidden years of preparation. Jesus must be about His Father's business and doing His Father's will. If that will involved eighteen hidden, laborious, tedious years, He would not give in to fleshly impatience but would obey with delight. "I desire to do your will, O my God; your law is within my heart" (Psalm 40:8). It should be remembered that in those times the trade of a carpenter was not considered dishonorable. It was a vocation from which many rose to become rabbis.

The meekness exhibited by Jesus in working as a carpenter is all the more remarkable in the light of His subsequent amazing miracles. He could have dazzled the world with the display of His supernatural power. Instead, He worked as hard as any other man in order that in all things He might be "made like his brothers" (Hebrews 2:17).

From our Lord's choice and pursuit of this occupation, three facts emerge.

HE EXEMPLIFIED THE NOBILITY OF LABOR

He saw no contradiction in the Lord of glory's standing in the saw pit cutting the thick logs into planks, or using a plane and hammer. In days when white-collar workers tend to despise those who work with their hands, contemplation of the life of Jesus during those silent years would correct such pride. He was a carpenter, a working man who earned

THE EARTHLY OCCUPATION OF CHRIST

His living, as His contemporaries, by manual skill. His was no forty-hour week but a twelve-hour day, doubtless with overtime as well.

If it was not beneath the Son of God to work as a tradesman, then surely it is beneath none of His children. Because He was no stranger to "the dust and sweat of toil," as the hymn asserts, "sons of labor are dear to Jesus," and He has imparted both dignity and nobility to a life of toil. If they only knew it, Jesus is the working man's friend, who from His own experience is able to sympathize with their trials.

HE EXHIBITED PERFECT WORKMANSHIP

An old tradition has it that Joseph was not a skilled tradesman. Be that as it may, it is certain that such a charge could not be laid at the door of his foster son. In work no less than in ethics His standard would be nothing less than perfection. Not without reason was it said of Him, "He hath done all things well" (Mark 7:37 KJV).

Justin Martyr, who lived shortly after the death of John the apostle, wrote of Jesus: "When He was among men He made ploughs and yokes and other farm implements." In His subsequent ministry Jesus aptly employed the figure of yoke and plough to illustrate His teaching. It is not difficult to imagine that farmers eagerly sought His yokes, for they were "easy," to use His term, and did not gall the necks of the oxen. One writer suggests that there was one shop in Nazareth where benches were made to stand on four legs, and doors to open and shut properly, for no second-rate work ever left His bench—near enough was not good enough for our great teacher.

HE OBTAINED PHYSICAL STRENGTH FOR FUTURE SERVICE

Never in human history were a man's physical frame and nervous system called upon to endure such unremitting strain as that imposed on our Lord during the three years of public ministry that climaxed in the cross. Only a physically perfect constitution could have supported such unceasing activity and expenditure of energy. When it was recorded on one occasion that He perceived "that power had gone out from him" (Mark 5:30), we are given an indication of the cost at which all of His ministry was carried out. The physical effort alone was enormous. His recorded journeys during the three years—and there is no reason to believe that all His journeys are included—cover at least 2,500 miles traveled on foot. He was usually thronged with people, and always preaching, teaching, and healing.

What better preparation could there be for such a demanding program than twelve hours a day spent in the saw pit or at the bench, planing and hammering, in the seclusion of Nazareth? These silent years He recognized as part of His Father's preparation, and they were invaluable in building up the physical and emotional reserves that were to be so heavily overdrawn in coming days that He would stagger under the weight of His own cross.

These considerations bring our Lord very near to us. Although we may not be able to emulate Him in His gracious ministry, it is open to us to follow Him in a life of faithful though perhaps hidden work. Like our Master, we can "do all to the glory of God" (1 Corinthians 10:31 KJV). We can appreciate the nobility of honest labor. We can welcome the years of quiet work that may be necessary to prepare us for public ministry.

KEY INSIGHT
INTO THE LIFE AND WORK OF CHRIST

The One who created the universe chose to live out His earthly life as a mere carpenter, earning His living by the sweat of His brow.

7

THE BAPTISM
OF CHRIST

The door of the carpenter's shop swung shut for the last time. Never again would children on their way home from school, drawn by the irresistible charm of the carpenter, pause to listen to one of His instructive stories.

Leaving His humble home (Mark 1:9), Jesus made His way toward the river Jordan, where enormous crowds were flocking. The center of interest was an ascetic and unusual preacher who was preaching repentance and administering baptism for the remission of sins. "Repent," he commanded, "for the kingdom of heaven is near" (Matthew 3:2). Here was a prophet after the order of Elijah, and just as fearless.

THE BAPTISMAL RITE

Pressing His way through the milling crowds seeking baptism at the hand of the prophet, the former carpenter humbly took His place among the candidates. When John the Baptist saw this holy and radiant face, he who had baptized so many others upon repenting of their sin was suddenly overwhelmed with an acute sense of his own sin and personal unworthiness. Not long before he had thundered at the Pharisees, "You brood of vipers! Who warned you to flee from the coming wrath?"

(Matthew 3:7). Now in abject humility he was saying to Jesus, "I need to be baptized by you, and do you come to me?" (Matthew 3:14). It was not appropriate that the Messiah should ask baptism at his hands. He had refused baptism to the Pharisees because of their lack of repentance. Now he wanted to refuse to administer it to Jesus because of his own sinfulness.

Jesus replied in words that assured John of the rightness of His submitting to this ritual cleansing. "'Let it be so now; it is proper for us to do this to fulfill all righteousness.' Then John consented" (Matthew 3:15). The fact that Jesus had done nothing needing repentance did not relieve Him of the obligation to complete this act of righteous obedience. True, He had no sins to confess, but He was a child of Abraham, and to submit to John's baptism was something God expected Him to do. It was an act of submission on the part of the perfect Man that was in complete harmony with the rest of His life. John then withdrew his opposition and administered the ordinance.

So the record shows. How much John previously knew of Jesus is not easy to determine, but there seems slender basis for the artists' legends that they were companions in early life. Nazareth and Hebron were widely separated. It is not impossible that they may have met on the annual Jerusalem pilgrimages. Be that as it may, he had been given a sign by which he could identify the Messiah. "The man on whom you see the Spirit come down and remain is he who will baptize with the Holy Spirit" (John 1:33). Was it the contrast between His strong, pure, holy face and the sinful appearances of the other candidates that convinced John this was indeed the Messiah?

This was the last act of our Lord's private life. Emerging from the waters of Jordan, He set out on His public ministry, empowered by the Spirit and assured of His Father's approval.

SIGNIFICANCE OF THE BAPTISMAL RITE

Why did Jesus seek baptism at the hands of John, whose baptism was primarily a purifying rite? In what sense could Jesus have part in a baptism involving repentance, when He had nothing of which to repent? Here is mystery indeed.

To the other candidates it carried a double meaning. It involved the acknowledgment and abandonment of their old sins. It signified entrance into the messianic era. To Jesus, the former element was absent. Baptism to Him was not the sacrament of repentance, nor is it so represented. With reference to the latter, it signified His entrance upon the new era of which He Himself was to be the founder, for His baptism was nothing less than "a sacramental recognition of Himself as Messiah."

IMPLICATIONS OF THE BAPTISMAL RITE

In His baptism and the accompanying circumstances we may see at least four implications.

His identification with the world's sin. By this act He allied Himself with the race He had come to redeem—the preliminary and necessary step to becoming the sinner's substitute. It signified His complete dedication of Himself to be the world's sin-bearer, yielding Himself without reserve to His Father's will even though it involved a cross. It was the public exhibition of His willingness to assume the burden of the sin of the whole race.

His baptism involved no acknowledgment of sin but only His purpose to be "made like his brothers" (Hebrews 2:17) in all things. Must the Levitical priest wash before he could minister at the altar? Then so will Jesus, for the new covenant has not yet begun. Is it prophesied of Him that He is to be "numbered with the transgressors" (Isaiah 53:12)? Then He will take His place with them in that symbol of death, even as He would finally associate Himself with them in actual death. Though sinless Himself, He was able to sympathize with His brethren in their struggle with sin.

His introduction into the messianic office. It was eminently fitting that so revolutionary a public ministry should be inaugurated by some such public ceremony as would clearly mark the watershed of His private and public life. By administering baptism to Him, the forerunner of the

Messiah set Him apart to His mission of redemption and sanctioned His claims.

With His knowledge of the Scriptures, it is impossible that Jesus did not realize the awful implications of the symbolism of this rite, foreshadowing as it did His own death and resurrection. Did He not say, "I have a baptism to undergo, and how distressed I am until it is completed" (Luke 12:50)? Yet, knowing all this, He gladly consecrated Himself to His costly life's purpose.

His Father's recognition of the silent years. Who can measure what the rending of the heavens meant to the Son of Man at this critical hour? With what balm would His Father's approving words fall on His spirit as they broke the silence of eternity: "You are my Son, whom I love; with you I am well pleased" (Luke 3:22)? Jesus was marked out as the One in whom the psalm found its fulfillment: "The Lord . . . said to me, 'You are my Son'" (Psalm 2:7), and He was declared by God to be perfectly qualified to embark on His public ministry.

His anointing for service. "The Holy Spirit descended on him in bodily form like a dove" (Luke 3:22). This was no meaningless display. From the moment of His conception until His self-sacrifice on the altar of the cross, everything was achieved "through the eternal Spirit" (Hebrews 9:14). Indeed that dependence on the Spirit characterized His entire ministry. His human nature was enabled to be the organ of the divine (John 3:34) by a peculiar gift of the Spirit bestowed on Him without measure at His baptism.

The phrase "in bodily form like a dove" may be rendered also as "in appearance as a dove." As fire is the most usual symbol of the divine presence, the Holy Spirit descended on Him as a flame of fire, falling on Him from heaven in the form of a dove, encircling and resting on Him. Whether this is so or not, the symbolism of the dove was entirely appropriate to the meekness and purity of the One on whom it rested —not a strong eagle but a gentle dove. Christ had come to conquer, not by force of arms but by love and humility.

Addressing the group gathered in the house of Cornelius, Peter recounted "how God anointed Jesus of Nazareth with the Holy Spirit and power, and how he went around doing good and healing all who were under the power of the devil, because God was with him" (Acts 10:38). Peter linked this anointing with His baptism by John, for the anointing of the Spirit occurred alongside His water baptism. By it He was endued with extraordinary power and the gifts necessary for His public ministry. Doubtless this event marked a distinct stage in His spiritual history as the Son of Man. Although in His case there was no need of cleansing, there was the necessity to learn "obedience from what he suffered" (Hebrews 5:8).

In this connection G. H. C. McGregor writes: "He was always well-pleasing to the Father; but I cannot read my New Testament without feeling that after this wonderful gift of the Spirit, His knowledge of the Father, His sympathy with the Father's purpose, His delight in His Father's will were deeper than ever. There was, of course, no change in His character, but there was growth, and it was this that fitted Him for His work. It was in virtue of what He became through His anointing at His baptism that He was able to do what He did."

This empowerment was not for Himself alone. It was for the sake of all who should believe on Him. "The one who sent me to baptize with water," says John, "told me, 'The man on whom you see the Spirit come down and remain is he who will baptize with the Holy Spirit'" (John 1:33). This was a gift, not for Christ alone but also for His church. We should therefore inquire of ourselves whether we are living in the full enjoyment of this heavenly gift. Have we through a similar submission and dedication to the Father's purpose experienced a comparable anointing for service?

It should be noted that in this incident there is clear revelation of the cooperation of the Trinity in preparing the way for our Lord's mediatorial work. *The incarnate Son* stands in the waters of Jordan, identifying Himself with sinful humanity. *The Father* opens heaven to voice His approval of His Son, whom He had selected for this task. *The Spirit* descends from heaven to empower the Son to fulfill the purpose of the Father.

KEY INSIGHT
INTO THE LIFE AND WORK OF CHRIST

*Although He had no sins to confess,
the baptism of Jesus was
an act of obedience
to prepare for the challenges
of His upcoming ministry.*

8

THE TEMPTATION
OF CHRIST

The words "At once the Spirit sent him out into the desert, and he was in the desert forty days, being tempted by Satan" (Mark 1:12–13) assure us that in the temptation of Christ the initiative was on the side of the divine, not the demonic.

After the approval of heaven at Jordan came the assault of hell; after the dove, the devil. This is the usual order in spiritual experience, and in this the Master was no exception. The fact that Jesus was full of the Spirit (Luke 4:1) did not exempt Him from the rigors of temptation. Does subtle temptation usually attack men at the threshold of their careers, the temptation to substitute the lower for the higher? Then in this, too, He will be "made like his brothers" (Hebrews 2:17).

A PERSONAL TEMPTER

An objective reading of the relevant Scriptures leaves no doubt that there was a personal agent in the Temptation—not a personification of evil, but an evil person with vast though restricted power. The language used cannot be made to fit an impersonal force or influence.

In the wilderness Jesus was not engaged merely in an inner conflict with His own desires and ambitions, but in a desperate, long, drawn-out struggle with the external adversary of God and man, the devil. It would be strange indeed if Satan were to allow the Messiah to engage in a mission that would result in his own overthrow without trying to deflect Him from His purpose.

The place where the Second Adam met and vanquished the tempter is in striking contrast to that in which the first Adam succumbed to his temptation—the arid wilderness, not the luxurious Eden. It should be noted that Jesus was tempted in solitude. The monastic life cannot save from satanic assaults.

Since Jesus was alone in the wilderness, He only could have given a report of what transpired, probably on an occasion when He was opening His heart to His intimate friends. We should be grateful to Him for preserving this record of His victory and of the principles on which we too may overcome.

TEMPTED IN ALL POINTS

Exactly what is implied in the statement that Jesus was "tempted in every way, just as we are" (Hebrews 4:15)? Does it mean that Jesus experienced every kind of temptation experienced by men and women of all ages? Obviously, no. He did not face the temptations peculiar to the space age, for example.

It means that temptation assailed Him in its full force along every avenue in which it can reach human nature. The surrounding circumstances and details of the temptation may differ, but temptations are essentially the same for all men and women in all ages. It would mean that Jesus was tempted in every part of His humanity, as we are.

Nor need it be assumed that the three recorded temptations were the only assaults the devil made on His holy soul during the forty days. These were only samples. Luke's account seems to imply this: "He ate nothing during those days, and *at the end of them* he was hungry" (Luke 4:2, italics added). He was tempted during the whole forty days, but He was so preoccupied with His spiritual challenge that He did not eat. It was at the end of the forty days that He became hungry. The three representative tests followed.

Leander S. Keyser has suggested that temptation can come to man along only three avenues. All other temptations are merely variants of these three.

Appetite: the desire to enjoy things. In his first letter, John refers to this as "the cravings of sinful man" (1 John 2:16).

Since Jesus was hungry, Satan made his first approach on the physical plane and in the realm of legitimate appetite. He came in the role of a benefactor. Why not turn these stones into bread? Desire for food is God-given and innocent. Since He was the Son of God, why not use His inherent power to gratify His legitimate desire? The temptation was so plausible that few if any of us would have detected in it a satanic attack.

The whole point of the test focused on *the Lord's submission to the will of God.* In each temptation Satan tried to induce Jesus to act in a manner contrary to complete dependence on God, by asserting a measure of independence springing from self-interest.

Jesus' method of meeting the fiery dart was simple, yet most effective. The Spirit who had led Him to this spot recalled to Him a relevant passage of Scripture that exposed the true nature of the temptation. "It is written: 'Man does not live on bread alone, but on every word that comes from the mouth of God'" (Matthew 4:4; cf. Deuteronomy 8:3). These words expressed His utmost confidence that His Father would supply Him with needed bread in His own way and time.

He refused to employ His divine power to gratify His own natural desires. To yield to the satanic suggestions would be tantamount to a denial of His incarnation, because He would be calling into His service powers which His brethren could not employ.

Further, it would have been satisfying a legitimate craving in an illegitimate way. He preferred remaining ravenously hungry to moving out of line with His Father's will. He would await His Father's word and provision. Had He yielded and provided Himself with bread by a miracle, His call to discipleship would have been out of the question for those who possessed no such powers but must earn their daily bread by the sweat of their brow.

Ambition: the desire to achieve things. This John designates "the pride of life" (1 John 2:16 KJV; "the boasting of what he has and does," NIV).

The scene changes. Satan takes Jesus up to one of the parapets of the temple. The pinnacle was in all probability the southern wing overlooking the Kidron Valley hundreds of feet below, the greatest depth well-known to the Jews. Josephus asserted that "anyone looking down would be giddy, while his sight would not reach to such an immense depth." Satan's suggestion was that Jesus should leap into this abyss, not into the crowded temple court.

The focus of this temptation was on His confidence in God, and the tempter supported his proposition by an apt quotation from Scripture, from which he omitted a vital phrase, "in all your ways" (Luke 4:10–11; cf. Psalm 91:11–12). Jesus was challenged to prove His faith by putting God's promise to the test.

The Master's reply clearly revealed that for Him to act in this way would be not faith but presumption. He avoided the peril of fanaticism, refusing to go beyond the limits God had laid down and tempting God, for God is not bound to respond to every irresponsible whim of our want of faith. The Jews sought a Messiah who would work dazzling wonders and establish a worldwide empire with Jerusalem as its center, and this was a temptation to yield to their carnal expectations.

Note the repeated use of "It is written" in Jesus' replies to the devil. Jesus knew how to wield the sword of the Spirit. He would not presumptuously place Himself in the way of danger but would always follow the will of His Father. He refused to attempt to dazzle people into faith. He would not establish His kingdom by display and outward show.

Foiled again, the tempter makes a last attempt to seduce Jesus.

Greed: the desire to obtain things, designated by John "the lust of [a person's] eyes" (1 John 2:16).

The first temptation was on the physical plane, the second on the mental. In the third, Satan invades the realm of the spiritual—giving to him a place that belongs to God alone.

This time he takes Jesus to a high mountain. Apparently in a vision, for "all the kingdoms of the world and the glory of them" (see Luke 4:5–6) could not be seen from any mountain in Palestine, and the glory of world domination was brought vividly before the Son of Man. Satan offered Him an outward kingdom with its outward splendor. Jesus did not challenge Satan's boast of the power to give Him the kingdoms of the world or charge him with falsehood.

Jesus had indeed come to obtain the power and glory of the whole world, but He was to receive it in His Father's way in His Father's time. And His Father's way included death on a cross. He perceived that Satan was offering Him the crown without the cross. The devil focused his last temptation on *the possibility of an evasion of the cross* by a compromise with him.

For the third time our Lord draws the sword of the Spirit from its sheath and wields it expertly. "Away from me, Satan! For it is written: 'Worship the Lord your God, and serve him only'" (Matthew 4:10).

Having failed to storm the fortress of Christ's loyalty and absolute obedience to His Father's will, the adversary departed from Him "for a season," but only for a season (Luke 4:13 KJV). Later he returned to the attack with greater fury.

The record implies that in each case Jesus heard the temptation from within but did not open the door to the tempter. In this way He gained a stunning victory over His enemy, the benefits of which can be shared today by every tempted soul. Because the Christ to whom we are united by faith was victorious over every class of temptation, we may share in His triumph as we appropriate it by faith.

Here is the essence of the three temptations:

1. The first was the temptation to satisfy a legitimate appetite by illegitimate means.
2. The second was the temptation to produce spiritual results by unspiritual means.
3. The third was the temptation to obtain a lawful heritage by unlawful means.

It is not without significance that each of the answers of Jesus to Satan was a quotation from the book of Deuteronomy. Our Lord thus stamped the Pentateuch as the Word of God.

Joseph Parker draws attention to some interesting features in the answers of our Lord to Satan's suggestions.

They were not the result of a keen intellectualism on the part of Christ to which we sinful humans may not lay claim.

They were not the outcome of ready wit nor of an unexpected flash of inspiration.

They do not bear the marks of inventive genius.

They were not answers that came on the spur of the moment as a result of His infinite wisdom.

They were not philosophical arguments elaborately stated and eloquently discussed.

But they were simple enough for the average child to understand.

They were quotations from the Word of God on which He meditated day and night.

They were authoritative, not in the form of submitted suggestions. Human reasonings and arguments are weak in conflicts with Satan because they lack authority.

THE ISSUE OF THE TEMPTATION

In relation to Christ, the Temptation ended in unqualified triumph. The suggestions of the Evil One left Him untainted by sin. His relationship with His Father remained undisturbed. He entered into the Temptation "full of the Holy Spirit." He returned "in the power of the Spirit" (Luke 4:1, 14), enriched, not impoverished, by the experience.

In relation to Satan, the Temptation meant total defeat. Each reply of Jesus dealt another stunning blow. His subtleties and deception were ruthlessly exposed. His defeat in the wilderness previewed his final and absolute defeat at the end of the age.

In relation to the believer, the Temptation victory gives assurance of the possibility of personal triumph over Satan and his wiles. It holds out the possibility of emerging from the bitterest temptation completely pure and in full confidence of our sonship. The weapon used by our Lord in the contest is equally available to the believer, so that he need not be "frightened in any way by those who oppose [him]" (Philippians 1:28).

KEY INSIGHT
INTO THE LIFE AND WORK OF CHRIST

The purpose of the
three temptations of Jesus
was to obtain beneficial results
by unlawful means,
but He overcame them
through the Word of God.

9

THE DEITY
OF CHRIST

I s any other question so far-reaching and important as the question, "Who was Jesus?" "Is He or is He not God?"

If Jesus is not God, then there is no viable Christianity, and we who worship Him are nothing more than idolaters. Conversely, if He is God, those who say He was merely a good man, or even the best of men, are blasphemers. More serious still, if He is not God, then *He* is a blasphemer in the fullest sense of the word. If He is not God, He is not even good.

The deity of Christ is the key doctrine of Scripture. Reject it, and the Bible becomes a confused jumble of words without any unifying theme. Accept it, and the Bible becomes an intelligible and ordered revelation of God in the person of Jesus Christ. Christ is the center of Christianity, and the conception we form of Christianity is therefore the conception we have of Him.

Our belief in the deity of Christ is, in the final analysis, based on our faith in the Scriptures. We believe Him to be the Son of God because we accept the teaching of Holy Scripture and its statements about Him. When we assert belief in the deity of Christ we mean that the person known to history as Jesus of Nazareth existed in eternity before He became man as the infinite and eternal God, the second person of the Trinity.

The very basis of Christianity is that Jesus was God manifest in the flesh (1 Timothy 3:16). If that assertion can be overthrown, then the whole superstructure of Christianity crashes to the ground, and we are bound to assume that Jesus was either a shameless impostor or that He suffered from a delusion. In either case He is disqualified from being our Savior, and the most potent factor in human existence, our salvation, is left entirely without credibility.

DEITY OR DIVINITY?

Two terms are used to express the Godhood of Christ, *deity* and *divinity.* Is there any significant difference in the meanings of the two words?

It is unfortunate that the latter term, which was considered synonymous with the former half a century ago, has been debased in meaning by liberal theologians and is now applied indifferently to both Christ and man. *Divinity* pertains to that which is celestial or supernatural in nature. *Deity* has only one proper meaning and pertains exclusively to the Trinity.

We may speak in a limited sense of the divinity of man since he was made in the image of God, but in no sense is it right to speak of the deity of man. It has become the practice among evangelical Christians to use the less easily misunderstood term *deity* to apply to our Lord. *Deity* implies that He has absolute equality with the Father, of whose person and glory He is the exact expression (Hebrews 1:3).

Bishop Handley Moule wrote in this context, "I well recognise the profound possible distinction between divinity and deity. With all possible conviction and faith I confess my Redeemer, the Lord Jesus Christ, on whom my whole hope of eternal life and present rest and strength depends, to be in the proper and ultimate sense, God, eternal, all-holy, almighty, one from and to eternity with the Father and the Spirit."

CREEDAL TESTIMONY

Creedal testimony to Christ's deity is found often, beginning with that first confession of Peter, which the Lord attributed not to keen spiritual insight but to divine revelation: "You are the Christ, the Son of the living God" (Matthew 16:16).

Here are three creedal statements:

The Apostles' Creed, dating back to A.D. 165, runs: "I believe in God the Father, Almighty, Maker of heaven and earth, and in Jesus Christ His only Son our Lord . . . ," a confession possible only to a true Christian.

The Nicene Creed (A.D. 325), formulated as it was to meet errors that had sprung up in the church, is even more explicit: "I believe . . . in one Lord Jesus Christ, the only begotten Son of God . . . being of one substance with the Father. . . ."

The Westminster Confession, now more than three centuries old, runs: "The Son of God, the second Person in the Trinity, being very and eternal God, of one substance, and equal with the Father did, when the fulness of time was come, take upon Him man's nature. . . ."

Throughout the centuries there has been an unbroken chain of creedal testimony to the Godhood of Christ.

PERSONAL TESTIMONY

While personal testimony is not in itself proof, it is significant that there is a volume of testimony on this point from unbelievers as well as believers.

Unbelievers have outdone each other in applauding the unique character of Christ, and in a court of law favorable evidence from a witness for the opposing side carries great weight. Here are some tributes from unbelievers and even enemies of Christianity.

Ernest Renan, the French heathen: "Repose now in Thy glory, noble founder. Thy work is finished! Thy divinity is established. . . . Between Thee and God there will no longer be distinction. . . . Whatever may be the surprises of the future, Jesus will never be surpassed."

Lord Byron, pleasure-loving poet: "If ever a man was God, or God was man, Jesus Christ was both."

J. J. Rousseau, immoral atheist: "If the life and death of Socrates were those of a sage, the life and death of Jesus were those of a God."

Napoleon, the ruthless conqueror: "I know men, and I tell you, Jesus was not a man. Superficial minds see a resemblance between Christ and the founders of empires and the gods of other religions. This resemblance does not exist. . . . Jesus Christ alone founded His Empire upon love, and at this hour millions would die for Him. In every other existence but that of Christ, how many imperfections."

Believers by the thousands have added their testimony and of these a few are selected.

Daniel Webster, American statesman: "I believe Jesus Christ to be the Son of God."

William Shakespeare, immortal poet: "Jesus Christ, my Savior."

William E. Gladstone, prime minister of Britain: "All that I live for is based on the divinity of Christ."

Alexander Whyte, Scottish preacher: "The longer I live, the firmer is my faith rooted in the Godhead of my Redeemer. No one short of the Son of God could meet my case. I must have one who is able to save to the utmost."

DENIALS OF CHRIST'S DEITY

It is a striking fact that it was not until the fourth century that there was a serious assault on the belief of Christians in the deity of Christ. Then it was Arius the noted heretic who led the attack. From the form his attack took, it is apparent that until then Christians had accepted the doctrine without question. His arguments were not raised to correct an existing heresy, but to overthrow the currently accepted view.

Without question, the last battle of the Christian age, as the first, will center in the person of Christ. It is significant that most of the modern religious cults are in error concerning the person and deity of Christ.

Spiritism asserts that "it is an absurd idea that Jesus was more divine than any other man."

Christian Science claims: "Jesus Christ is not God, as Jesus Himself declared, but the Son of God."

Jehovah's Witnesses boldly state: "Jesus was not God the Son."

Being thus in error at the center, these and other similar cults cannot but be wrong at the circumference.

THE WITNESS OF SCRIPTURE

The four Gospels are, of course, the main source of our knowledge of the person of our Lord. The Old Testament, however, also makes its contribution to the subject. References to Jehovah in the Old Testament are applied to Christ in the New. That is unwarranted if He was not God. Yet, as strict monotheists, the New Testament writers constantly use these terms without any explanation or apparent awareness of any contradiction. In illustration of this, compare Matthew 3:3 with Isaiah 40:3; Ephesians 4:7–8 with Psalm 68:18; and 1 Peter 2:8 with Isaiah 8:14.

The four evangelists are obviously depicting a real and not an imaginary character. It has been suggested that they created the story out of their own imaginations, but that assumption is incredible. How could those "unlearned and ignorant men" (Acts 4:13 KJV) with such skill invent such an incomparable figure? You might as well expect four artists to take up palette and brush and combine to produce a masterpiece in art eclipsing a Raphael!

Again, the moral and religious atmosphere in which those men lived was entirely hostile to the message they recorded. How could provincial, exclusive Jews, with their scorn of the Gentiles, paint such a glowing portrait of a Messiah whose love embraced both Jew and Gentile?

To contend that the Christ of the Bible is the offspring of mere human imagination and had no historical reality would make the Gospels as great a miracle in the realm of literature as the living Christ is in the realm of history. Ernest Renan remarked that it would take a Jesus to invent a Jesus.

The gospel narratives are so thoroughly saturated with the assumption of His deity that it crops out in quite unexpected ways and places. In three passages in Matthew's record, for example, He is represented as speaking most naturally of "his angels" (Matthew 13:41; 16:27; 24:31).

The four Gospels combine to present a character absolutely unique, the one universal perfect Man. Each Gospel presents identically the same character. The Christ of Mark says and does nothing inconsistent with the Christ of Matthew. And more remarkable still, the New Testament epistles continue to present "this same Jesus."

CHRIST'S POWERS AND PREROGATIVES

The attributes of deity are ascribed to Him in the Scriptures.

He Himself laid claim to *omnipotence.* "All authority in heaven and on earth has been given to me" (Matthew 28:18). On occasions He exhibited this power over nature (Matthew 8:27), over demons (Luke 4:36), over angels (Matthew 26:53), over disease (Luke 4:40), and over death (Mark 5:41–42).

Omniscience is implied in the statement "Jesus would not entrust himself to them, for he knew all men" (John 2:24; see also John 4:29; 16:30; Colossians 2:3).

The promise connected to our Lord's Great Commission involves the *omnipresence* of Christ. "Surely I am with you always, to the very end of the age" (Matthew 28:20).

He asserted His own *self-existence* in these words: "As the Father has life in himself, so he has granted the Son to have life in himself" (John 5:26; see also John 8:57–58; Revelation 1:8).

Actions are ascribed to Christ that are possible to the Deity alone: creation (Colossians 1:16; Hebrews 1:10), resurrection (John 5:28–29), and judgment (John 5:27).

When Thomas exclaimed, "My Lord and my God!" (John 20:28), Jesus did not rebuke him for blasphemy but accepted his claim of deity without hesitation. Contrast this with the reaction of the angel when John fell down to worship him: "Do not do it!" (Revelation 22:8–9).

In reviewing the claims Christ made, we are faced with three possibilities: *(a)* He was a deceiver and was not telling the truth. But that is contradicted by His whole life and work. *(b)* He was self-deceived and thought such things of Himself, but they had no basis in fact. But the fact that He performed miracles and that He was raised from the dead contradict that. *(c)* The third and only reasonable possibility is that He was exactly what He claimed to be.

THE WITNESS OF CHRIST'S CLAIMS

No other man in history has made claims for himself that parallel those made by Christ.

He showed a sublime self-awareness of His own person and work. Christ preached Himself. "He distinctly, repeatedly, energetically preaches Himself," says Canon H. P. Liddon. The fact that He was "meek and lowly in heart" (Matthew 11:29 KJV), and that He sought nothing for Himself, gives additional emphasis to this tremendous self-assertion. In anyone else it would have been absurd and blasphemous, but in Him it does not seem false.

In the first words recorded of Him, He offsets the words "my Father" against His mother's "your father" (Luke 2:41–52), surely an indication of His awareness of a unique relation existing between Himself and God.

To the horror of the Jews, He even went so far as to assume to Himself the sacred divine name—"I AM." "Before Abraham was born, I am!" (John 8:58; cf. Exodus 3:14). In point of fact, no fewer than sixteen names clearly implying deity are used of the Lord, as, for example, "Lord of glory."

No less astounding are the claims He made in His "I AM" utterances (John 6:35; 8:12; 10:7–11). These are undoubted assumptions of deity, as is His claim to possess the divine resources to meet all human need (Matthew 11:28; John 4:14; 7:37–38; 10:28).

He manifested a superhuman character. The grandeur of His character added confirmation to His claims. He was too sincere to prefer a false claim, too humble and unselfish to seek selfish honor.

His disciples, who had ample opportunity to observe His inner life, never found Him to fail. They were impressed by His moral courage and amazed at His miracles. It was out of daily conversation as well as divine illumination that Peter's confession was spoken: "You are the Christ, the Son of the living God."

He assumed superiority over prior revelation. Concerning the attitude of the Lord to the Old Testament Scriptures, D. M. McIntyre has this to say: "The Sermon on the Mount is a summary of the ethical teachings of the Old Testament. And our Lord, with all His profound reverence for Scripture, holds Himself towards it with a certain freedom. He clears away rabbinical glosses (Matthew 5:43); He affirms the transitory and imperfect nature of the civil law in Israel (Matthew 5:31); He shows that the divine pronouncement reaches beneath the letter of the statute, and searches the thoughts and intents of the heart (Matthew 5:21). He brings all life under His personal rule; the test of conduct is 'for my sake' (Matthew 5:11)."

As a final word of authority, His often-repeated "Verily, I say unto you" (KJV; "I tell you the truth," NIV) in the Gospels was nothing short of an assertion of a divine authority.

THE WITNESS OF
THE SPREAD OF CHRISTIANITY

Christianity is the greatest proof of Christ's deity, because He as its Head measures up to the highest standard of deity. Although the Scriptures are the greatest testimony to the deity of Christ, there are other avenues of evidence. Think of the mighty revolution He has caused in the world. The growth and spread of other religions can be traced to natural causes, but Christianity can be accounted for only by supernatural causes.

To compare Christianity with Islam is impossible, for Islam made its tremendous advances by the sword and continues to gain adherents by condoning sin instead of condemning it. Like its fellow religions, it is mainly confined to the nations in or near to the region in which it had its birth.

How different it is with Christianity, which knows no distinction of race or creed but claims the world for Christ and whose messengers circle the globe. Where it comes and is faithfully practiced, sin and slavery and selfishness are banished and holiness is enthroned.

From where comes this universality and ability to capture the hearts of men of every race and culture? Could this transforming influence, still undiminished, have proceeded from a mere man?

THE WITNESS OF
CHRIST'S TRANSFORMING POWER

Christ's ministry of power is another link in the already strong chain of proof of His deity. What gained for Him the unquestioning obedience and unfaltering loyalty of His followers? If He be not the Son of God, how can we explain the fact that after two millennia there are millions who would gladly surrender life itself rather than deny Him? The transformed lives of Christians are an eloquent and ever-present witness to the deity of the person from whom the transforming power proceeds.

KEY INSIGHT
INTO THE LIFE AND WORK OF CHRIST

The very basis of our faith is that Jesus Christ was fully God revealed in the flesh, and the Scriptures continually attest to it in various ways.

10

THE HUMANITY
OF CHRIST

The Son of Man." "The Man Christ Jesus." How close those titles bring our Lord to us! The reality of His human nature links Him with the whole human race. It assures us of His unfailing interest and sympathy. Although we must not divorce the humanity from the deity of the Master, we should draw all the comfort and help we can from the fact that He took part in historic manhood and was made "in the likeness of sinful man" (Romans 8:3). We can rejoice with one of the early Fathers that "He who is always, before all ages, perfect God, became Himself perfect man at the end of the days for us, and for our salvation." Within Himself He holds those two natures in perfect balance. His humanity was real and not imposture. It was genuine and not faulty.

The early Christians prostrated themselves in adoration as they recalled the descent of the Son of God to the lowliness of our nature and the pressure of our need. D. M. McIntyre writes, "There was in the Church a tendency to think less seriously of the true humanity of our Lord. The complaint of a master of theology, 'We allow His humanity to hide His deity,' is deprived of its point in our day: we are so deeply absorbed in our Lord's life of manhood in the flesh that we are apt to ignore, if not to question His very deity. But in the sub-apostolic period it was otherwise."

DENIAL OF CHRIST'S REAL HUMANITY

The writers of the four Gospels were never in doubt of the reality of Christ's humanity, but this doctrine has not been undisputed in the history of the church. Appolinarius, Bishop of Laodicea, denied the existence of a rational soul in Christ's human nature. Regarding the soul as the seat of sin, he argued that therefore the sinless Son of Man could not have possessed a human soul.

In our own day Christian Science pursues a similar line. "Christ is incorporeal, spiritual," wrote Mary Baker Eddy in her *Miscellaneous Writings,* thus denying the reality of His body and His real humanity. John trenchantly denounced this heresy. "Every spirit that confesseth not that Jesus Christ is come in the flesh is not of God: and this is that spirit of antichrist" (1 John 4:3 KJV).

PROOF OF CHRIST'S REAL HUMANITY

In contrast to those heretical denials, let us examine the definite teaching of Scripture on the subject.

Details of His *human ancestry* are carefully preserved in the gospel records. He was born of the Virgin Mary, and "as to his human nature was a descendant of David" (Romans 1:3; cf. Acts 13:23). The names of His brothers are given, and His genealogy on both sides of the family is given in detail.

He was normal in His *human appearance*. So far as the woman of Samaria was concerned, at first Jesus was only another hated Jew. She noted nothing unusual in His appearance (John 4:9). To the two dispirited disciples trudging along the Emmaus road, He was only another fellow citizen, strangely out of touch with recent events (Luke 24:18). Even after the Resurrection when Jesus appeared in His glorified body, Mary at first mistook Him for the gardener (John 20:15). His own intimate friends mistook Him for another man when they returned from their fishing expedition (John 21:4–5). These incidents all combine to underline the natural and human qualities of His physical appearance.

So far as the essential elements of His *human capacities* were concerned, He possessed the normal powers and faculties of a man. He spoke of His body. "When she poured this perfume on my *body*, she did it to prepare me for burial" (Matthew 26:12). He referred to His soul. "My *soul* is overwhelmed with sorrow to the point of death" (Matthew 26:38). He spoke of His spirit. "Father, into your hands I commit my *spirit*" (Luke 23:46). These elements are essential to humanity. "May your whole *spirit, soul* and *body* be kept blameless," wrote Paul (1 Thessalonians 5:23, italics added).

When addressing Thomas, Jesus appealed to the normality of His human nature as a basis for belief. "Look at my hands and my feet. It is I myself! Touch me and see" (Luke 24:39). We must be careful to distinguish between "human nature" and "sinful nature." They are not synonymous, for Christ never possessed the latter, only the former. *Sin is not a necessary element in human nature*. It is a satanic intrusion.

As to His *human reputation*, Jesus called Himself "Son of Man" thirty times in Matthew, fourteen times in Mark, twenty-five times in Luke, and eleven times in John—eighty times in all. He wanted to be thought of as linked with man. By that title He claimed to be the representative of all humanity. Even when acquiescing in the title "Son of God," sometimes He immediately afterward substituted the title "Son of Man," as though to emphasize His possession of two natures in the unity of His person (e.g., John 1:49–51; Matthew 26:63–64). Then, too, He was called "man" by others; for example, see Acts 2:22; 1 Corinthians 15:21.

Augustus Strong has this to say concerning Christ's claim to be the Son of Man: "Consider what is implied in your being a man. How many parents had you? You answer, two. How many grandparents? You answer, four. How many great-grandparents? Eight. So the number of your ancestors increases as you go back, and if you take in only twenty generations, you will reckon yourself as the outcome of more than a million progenitors. . . . What is true of you was true on the human side of the Lord Jesus. In Him the lives of our common humanity converge. He was the Son of Man far more than He was the Son of Mary."

He displayed *human infirmities* and was moved by instincts normal

73

to human beings. The gospel records afford satisfying evidence that Jesus was subject to all the ordinary *sinless* infirmities of our human nature. There is not a note in the great organ of our humanity which, when touched, does not find a sympathetic vibration in the mighty scope and range of our Lord's being, except, of course, the jarring discord of sin.

Like every other man, He *hungered* (Mark 11:12). But God does not hunger (Psalm 50:12). After days of strenuous work He was *weary* (John 4:6). But God is never weary (Isaiah 40:28). He *slept* (Matthew 8:24). But God neither slumbers nor sleeps (Psalm 121:4). He was moved by human sympathy and *wept* (John 11:35). He *craved human sympathy* Himself (Matthew 26:36–40). He was tempted (Hebrews 4:15). But God cannot be tempted (James 1:13). He died (John 19:30). But God cannot die.

Our Lord's consenting to be subject to *human limitations* was part of the mystery of His great self-humiliation. While in His incarnate state He did not renounce His divine powers, His intelligence was so subject to human limitations that He submitted to the ordinary laws of human development. He was no exception. As noted in an earlier chapter, He acquired His knowledge through the ordinary channels open to the other boys of His day: through instruction, study, and reflection. It would appear that He even voluntarily renounced knowledge of certain future events. "No one knows about that day or hour, not even the angels in heaven, nor the Son, but only the Father" (Mark 13:32).

Like ourselves, Jesus was *not self-sustained* but needed prayer and communion with His Father for the support of His spiritual life. In all the great crises of His life, He resorted not to the counsel of men but to prayer to His Father for guidance (e.g., Luke 5:16; 6:12; 9:18, 28). He was subject to *human limitations of power.* He obtained the power for His divine works not by drawing on His inherent deity but by depending on the anointing Spirit (Acts 10:38).

One of the strongest evidences of the reality of His humanity was His experience of *human suffering.* He knew the salty taste of pain. Every nerve of His body was racked with anguish. Though He was God's Son, He was not exempt from suffering (Hebrews 5:8). His sufferings of body and of spirit have formed the theme of many books. The fact that He was sinless made Him more sensitive to pain than His sinful con-temporaries. We read of His being in agony. The events of His death on the cross assure us of His ability to sympathize with human suffering.

He displayed the ultimate in *human perfections.* By friend and foe He is acknowledged as the only perfect Man. All attempts to depict a per-fect character other than those of the four evangelists have been marred by the unmistakable evidences of the imperfections of the author. To con-ceive and portray a perfect character is beyond the powers of fallible man.

Then how could these Galilean fishermen conceive such a life? The simple answer is that they did not. They merely recorded faithfully the life of One who had lived in their midst and whose inmost life had been open to their scrutiny as they were in daily contact with Him.

If any fact stands out crystal clear in the New Testament, it is the com-plete and genuine humanity of Jesus Christ.

KEY INSIGHT
INTO THE LIFE AND WORK OF CHRIST

Even Jesus in His manhood needed the power of prayer and continual fellowship with His Father in order to sustain His spiritual life.

11

THE MANLINESS
OF CHRIST

Jesus was not only a man, He was the crown and glory of humanity. Scant justice has been done to the Master by the many artists who have attempted to interpret Him on canvas. He has far more frequently been represented as womanly and weak than as masculine.

It is certainly true that Jesus was a GENTLE-man, but He was none the less a gentle-MAN. He combined in Himself the gentler graces of womanhood and the virile virtues of manhood. Unfortunately it is the former that have received stronger emphasis.

When World War I was over, a sentence in the report of the chaplains of the services confirmed this impression. It said, "The average Tommy believed that Jesus was just and good but just a trifle soft." They never knew that He was Lion of Judah as well as Lamb of God.

A young man was being counseled by a Christian man when a conversation as follows ensued:

"I do not admire your Jesus. He was rather weak and effeminate. I like a man with red blood in his veins."

"I suppose you heard the usual Bible stories when you were younger?"

"Oh, yes, I used to love them as a child."

"And I suppose the rugged Elijah who appeared dramatically and fearlessly before the King of Israel and challenged the whole nation would be one of your favorite characters?"

"You have guessed right. I always admired his manliness."

"And in the New Testament, John the Baptist with his unconventional garb and fearless preaching would also attract you?"

"Strangely enough, you have lighted on my two favorite Bible characters."

"Then would it surprise you to know that when Jesus asked His disciples who men said He was, they replied, 'Some say that thou art John the Baptist: some, Elijah' (Matthew 16:14)? If He had been weak and effeminate as you contend, would they have been likely to confuse him with the rugged Elijah or the fearless Baptist?"

"I had never thought of that before."

Nor perhaps have many of us thought of Him like this.

We may feel with J. A. Broadus that the term *manliness* is inadequate. Yet it does help to impress on us an important element in the Savior's character, for people are inclined to think that goodness, innocence, patience, and purity belong to feeble characters, when the fact is far otherwise.

The manliness of Jesus can be seen in the following characteristics of His life and ministry.

HIS RESOLUTE COURAGE

Jesus knew more of peril than most, and yet when faced with it He never showed the slightest timidity or fear. The highest form of courage is not that of the blind enthusiast who in a moment of exaltation runs great risks, but that of the man who though clearly foreseeing the consequences of his action, nevertheless continues unwavering.

Though Jesus knew Jerusalem meant for Him suffering and death—and no one ever shrank from death as He did—yet "he stedfastly set his face to go to Jerusalem" (Luke 9:51 KJV). When confronted with the traitor and the rabble that accompanied him, Jesus refused to exercise the divine power He demonstrated on them to bring about deliverance. Rather, He invited them to take Him. He faced the suffering and shame of the cross with manly courage (John 12:27–28; 18:3–8). He displayed no fear of disease, of demons, or of men.

HIS INTREPID UTTERANCES

He is a strong man who will voluntarily speak words that must inevitably bring on him dire and painful consequences. And yet the Lord never withheld, from fear of possible consequences, one word given to Him by His Father.

Hear Him reply to Annas, "I have spoken openly to the world. . . . I said nothing in secret. Why question me? Ask those who heard me" (John 18:20–21). His reply to Pilate was equally fearless (John 18:33–37; 19:11).

HIS PHYSICAL ENDURANCE

Have you ever endeavored to calculate the extent of His travels or the magnitude of His labors during His brief ministry? In the many tours recorded in the Gospels as previously stated, it is estimated that He traveled on foot some 2,500 miles during the three years, and we need not conclude that every journey was recorded. Those were not unbroken marches, for He constantly stopped to help and heal, to teach and preach.

Ponder the strain imposed on His physique by the constant demands of the crowds milling around Him. Consider the constant drain on His nervous resources. We are apt to overlook the fact that He always helped others at His own expense. Even when the woman quietly touched the hem of His garment, it is recorded that "power had gone out from him" (Mark 5:30). It was costly service. Only a man with an extraordinary physique could have endured such relentless strain.

HIS COURAGEOUS SILENCE

It is often easier to speak than to keep silent. A strong man may be recognized by his silence, and this was true of the Master. He knew when to speak and when to hold His peace. However strong the provocation,

He never stooped to self-vindication, much less retaliation. Before the cynical Pilate and the taunting Herod, both of whom possessed the power of life and death, He maintained a majestic silence. His silences were often more eloquent than His speech (Matthew 26:62–63; 27:12; Mark 15:4–5; Luke 23:9).

HIS UNBENDING STERNNESS

Nothing is more awe-inspiring than the unbending severity of a kind man who has been roused to moral indignation. A man who is not tenderhearted becomes harsh and cruel. One who is only tenderhearted is weakly sentimental. But mercy and justice met and were harmonized in the character of the Son of Man.

Consider the bearing of the divine Lord as He enters His Father's house, which He loved so fervently, only to find it desecrated, "a den of thieves" (Luke 19:46 KJV). Watch the flashing of His eye, the resolute step as He advances with uplifted whip of cords and begins to oust the rapacious traffickers. Watch Him overturn the bankers' tables. "It is written, . . . 'My house will be a house of prayer,'" He is saying, "but you have made it 'a den of robbers'" (vv. 45–47).

In this incident we are given a graphic example of "the goodness and severity of God" (Romans 11:22 KJV; "kindness and sternness of God," NIV). Our Lord demonstrated not only moral courage but no small degree of physical bravery as well.

HIS REMARKABLE SELF-CONTROL

Not even once did Jesus betray the slightest semblance of lack of self-control. Strong though His emotions were, He always held them on a tight leash. Calm power and self-possession marked all His words and actions. "Now and then we meet a strong man," wrote R. E. Speer, "who has control over his emotions in the way of repression, and to some little extent of stimulation also, but generally there is a large range of involuntary and uncontrolled emotions which are true and unconscious

revelations of the inner life which they express and manifest, or betray.
... In Jesus there was no contradiction between the voluntary and the involuntary, the unconscious and the controlled. All the manifestations of His inner life were reliable and true, and they constantly increase our awe of Him and our sense of His majesty and mystery."

HIS STINGING DENUNCIATIONS

The tendency of our day is to overemphasize the love of God and Christ. A preacher who is unafraid to denounce in strong terms the sins of the day, within and without the church, is termed "un-Christlike."

But listen to these sentences from the lips of the King of love. "Woe unto you, scribes and Pharisees, hypocrites! for ye devour widows' houses, and for a pretence make long prayer: therefore ye shall receive the greater damnation. Woe unto you . . . for ye compass sea and land to make one proselyte, and when he is made, ye make him twofold more the child of hell than yourselves. . . . Woe unto you . . . for ye are like unto whited sepulchres, which indeed appear beautiful outward, but are within full of dead men's bones, and of all uncleanness. . . . Ye serpents, ye generation of vipers, how can ye escape the damnation of hell?" (Matthew 23:14–15, 27, 33 KJV).

It should be noted that those stinging words were not spoken to the Prodigal Son or to Mary Magdalene, but to the hypocritical ruling class and religious leaders. There are surely no soft effeminate qualities here.

HIS UNCOMPROMISING FRANKNESS

Christ never concealed the cross to gain a disciple. No one ever left all and followed Him who did not have opportunity to count the cost. His followers must be intelligent volunteers. The emphasis of our day is rather on what one gains by becoming a Christian. Jesus never failed to emphasize the cost of following Him. The birds had their nests, the foxes their holes, "but the Son of Man has no place to lay his head" (Matthew

8:20). Following Christ involves a love for Him transcending that for father or mother, wife or child. "Anyone who does not carry his cross and follow me *cannot* be my disciple" (Luke 14:27, italics added).

In His final agony, with tongue parched, fever raging, and joints dislocated, He was offered a sedative to deaden His sufferings. "They offered Jesus wine to drink, mixed with gall; but after tasting it, he refused to drink it" (Matthew 27:34). He displayed no unmanly shrinking from suffering. He showed Himself every inch a manly man in life's most testing hours.

KEY INSIGHT
INTO THE LIFE AND WORK OF CHRIST

Jesus exhibited the epitome of the best qualities of manhood in His courage, self-control, endurance, and other virtues.

12

THE TWOFOLD
NATURE OF CHRIST

The great American statesman Daniel Webster was dining with a company of literary men in Boston. The conversation turned upon Christianity. As the occasion was in honor of Mr. Webster, he was expected to take a leading part in the conversation, and he frankly stated his belief in the Godhead of Christ and his own dependence on His atonement.

A Unitarian minister opposite him responded. "Mr. Webster, can you comprehend how Jesus Christ could be both God and man?"

"No, sir, I cannot understand it," replied Webster, "and I would be ashamed to acknowledge Him as my Savior if I could comprehend it. He could be no greater than myself, and such is my conviction of accountability to God, my sense of sinfulness before Him, and my knowledge of my own incapacity to recover myself, that I feel I need a superhuman Savior."

The great confessions of the church affirm this as one of the cardinal Christian doctrines. Here are two examples.

> He continues to be God and man, in two distinct natures and one person for ever.
>
> Westminster Shorter Catechism

We confess that He is Very God and Very Man;
Very God by His power to conquer death and
Very Man that He might die for us.

Belgic Confession

It is just as heretical to affirm the deity of our Lord while omitting the reality of His humanity as it is to affirm the humanity while omitting the deity.

As we think of the union of the divine and human natures in the single personality of Jesus Christ—*hypostatic union,* or one person, as the theological term states it—we are at once confronted with mystery.

IT IS MYSTERIOUS

"Without controversy great is the mystery of godliness: God was manifest in the flesh," said Paul (1 Timothy 3:16 KJV). In this connection W. Graham Scroggie wrote: "Christ was human and divine; but we must not think of these as being distinct and separate in Him. Their relation must remain to us a mystery, but the evidence of each is abundant, and the necessity for both is obvious. Had He not been man, He could not have sympathized with us; and had He not been God, He could not have saved us."

The reason for the mystery is that we have no analogies to it in our own nature or experience. It is a truth of revelation that like many others must be accepted by faith, awaiting the dawn of eternal day for fuller knowledge, for a full explanation. The fact that there is mystery need not prevent us from taking at their full value the Scriptures that teach it.

Must we reject the doctrine of the Trinity, so clearly taught in the Scriptures, merely because to our minds it is an impenetrable mystery?

IT IS ACTUAL

Jesus was truly God; whatever it is to be God, Jesus was that absolutely. He was equally really man. His deity and His humanity were distinct and separate, and each nature retained its normal attributes. The divine did not permeate the human, nor was the human absorbed by the divine. St. Leo expressed it: "He united the true 'form of a servant' in which He was equal to God the Father, and combined both natures in a league so close that the lower was not consumed by receiving glory, nor the higher lessened by assuming lowliness."

The Son of God was not changed into a human being, nor did the man Jesus rise to a state of deity. The two natures were so bound as to constitute them a single undivided person, acting with a single mind and will. Since the union of the natures was accomplished without the conversion or weakening of either, Jesus Christ cannot be spoken of as God and man. He was the God-man.

Although He possessed those separate and distinct natures, He did not act sometimes by His human and sometimes by His divine nature only. He acted in all things as a single person. He is asleep in the stern of the boat, wearied with His day's service. In a moment He arises and controls the raging storm. Thus the reality of His humanity is seen against the background of His divine power and prerogatives.

Chrysostom has a striking paragraph on this theme: "I do not think of Christ as God alone, or man alone, but both together. For I know He was hungry, and I know that with five loaves He fed five thousand. I know He was thirsty, and I know that He turned the water into wine. I know He was carried in a ship, and I know that He walked on the sea. I know that He died, and I know that He raised the dead. I know He was set before Pilate, and I know that He sits with the Father on His throne. I know that He was worshiped by angels, and I know that He was stoned by the Jews. And truly some of these I ascribe to the human and others to the divine nature. For by reason of this He is said to have been both God and Man."

IT IS DEMONSTRABLE

In all His ministry our Lord uniformly speaks and is spoken of as a single person. There is no interchange of "I" and "You" between Christ's two natures, such as is recorded of the three persons of the Trinity (e.g.,

"I in them and you in me," John 17:23). Nor does He ever use the plural in speaking of Himself.

It is significant that the powers and attributes of both natures are ascribed to the one personality. We can attribute to the one person what is really appropriate to only one of the two natures; for example, "None of the rulers of this age understood [this], for if they had, they would not have crucified the Lord of glory" (1 Corinthians 2:8).

When we think of our Lord's ministry and life on earth, we make no distinction such as saying that a certain act or saying was divine and another purely human. Both proceeded from the single personality of Jesus Christ.

Again, Jesus spoke of Himself as being in heaven and on earth at the same time. "He that came down from heaven, even the Son of man which is in heaven" (John 3:13 KJV). This is unexplainable on any other theory than that the two natures were so organically united as to form a single person. "His Son, who was descended from David according to the flesh and designated Son of God in power according to the Spirit of holiness by his resurrection from the dead, Jesus Christ our Lord" (Romans 1:3–4 RSV).

IT IS NECESSARY

The value of the Atonement is intelligible only upon the assumption that the two natures were so united in Christ *that what each did had the value of both*. Had Christ been only man, His death would have meant no more than that of any other martyr who gave himself for others. Had He been only divine, He would have had no real link with humanity, and His death would have been devoid of any redeeming quality.

In the union of the two natures, the Atonement becomes not only available but infinite in its effects. Apart from it, Christ could not have been a proper mediator between God and man. His twofold nature enables Him to lay His hand on both—His deity affords Him equal dignity with God; His humanity gives Him perfect sympathy with man (Hebrews 2:17–18; 4:15–16).

But suppose He had been only human. How could He have helped us? He would have given us an inspiring example of how to live, but

His sympathy with us would have been of little avail. We need not only human sympathy but divine power. Assured of His human sympathy, we know that He is *willing* to help and save us. Assured of His divine power, we know that He is *able* to help and save us. This willingness and ability combine to make Him our all-sufficient Savior (Hebrews 7:25).

IT IS ETERNAL

It seems clear from Scripture that the Son of God assumed forever the humanity of which He partook at His birth. His incarnation is on-going. He could not lay aside His humanity without ceasing to be the Son of Man. This does not imply that He is forever subject to the natural limitations of life on this earth but that He has a bodily form manifested to His disciples after His resurrection. He never will cease to have all the essential attributes of humanity.

In the ascension of Christ, humanity attained the throne of the universe. His ascension appearances represent Him as having a literal but glorified body (Acts 7:56; 9:4–6; Revelation 1:9–18). "May we not believe," wrote D. M. McIntyre, "that the Holy Spirit holds in an indissoluble unity the human and the divine nature of our Lord. . . . The Spirit . . . was the Bond of Union between the divine and human natures of the Son."

KEY INSIGHT
INTO THE LIFE AND WORK OF CHRIST

The two natures of Christ
are distinct and separate,
and the lower human nature is
not consumed by His divine glory,
nor is His glory diminished
by His human lowness.

13

THE SINLESSNESS
OF CHRIST

There was a time in the history of the church when the sinlessness of Jesus was almost universally conceded, but that is not so today. This fundamental truth of Christianity has been denied by many intellectual critics. It is argued that on philosophical grounds there is an improbability of such a perfect life as that portrayed in the Gospels. We should be compelled to admit the validity of this objection if deity is left out of account.

The presence of a sinless man among universally sinful men would be as much a miracle in the moral realm as would a virgin birth in the physical realm. But in spite of this improbability, if sufficient evidence is given, is it reasonable to reject it? And we submit that sufficient evidence has been given.

Other objectors assert that since we have no record of the thirty years of obscurity, it is impossible to claim sinlessness when we are ignorant of His actions. To this we answer that we prove Christ's deity and base His sinlessness on that fact. Further, the claim is confirmed by those who lived closest to Him and were thus in the best position to know. The quality of His life during the thirty hidden years is best evidenced by the life He lived during His years of public ministry.

Sinlessness in Jesus was not merely a neutral quality of innocence as it was in the first Adam. "The New Testament speaks of His overcoming temptation," writes T. C. Edwards, "and temptation means nothing if it does not comprise striving against sin. The words 'in all points tempted like as we are, yet without sin' must mean that, although He was tempted to sin, the conflict left Him immaculate."

Jesus as High Priest is described as being "holy, blameless, pure, set apart from sinners" (Hebrews 7:26). He was holy in character, utterly devoted to God. He was guileless in the sense of being free from malice or baseness. He was undefiled, free from all moral impurity and defilement; He was separate—set apart permanently—from the sinners for whom He lived and died.

Consider the testimony to His sinlessness.

THE WITNESS OF SCRIPTURE

The fifteenth of the thirty-nine articles of faith of the Church of England sets out clearly a truth that finds consistent support in the Scriptures:

> Christ, in the truth of our nature was made like unto us in all things, sin only except, from which He was clearly void, both in His flesh and in His spirit.

There is not one statement of Scripture which, consistently interpreted, can be made to imply less than sinlessness for our Lord. Four affirmations by different New Testament writers are unequivocal in their testimony:

"In him is no sin" (1 John 3:5).
"He committed no sin" (1 Peter 2:22).
"[He] had no sin" (2 Corinthians 5:21).
"Tempted . . . yet was without sin" (Hebrews 4:15).

THE WITNESS OF CHRIST HIMSELF

The challenge flung out to His critics by the Lord still remains unanswered, "Can any of you prove me guilty of sin?" (John 8:46). His sinlessness was unimpeachable, or they would have brought a charge against Him. Even hell could bring no accusation. "The prince of this world is coming. He has no hold on me," Jesus claimed (John 14:30).

A study of His life reveals a consistent sense of immunity from sin. Never did He show the slightest discontent with Himself—a grave fault in any other man. Never did He shed a tear over conscious failure. He demanded repentance of others, yet was never penitent Himself. Nor can this self-satisfaction be explained on the grounds that His standard of duty or sense of moral obligation was less exacting than that of His contemporaries. The reverse was the case. His code of ethics was immeasurably higher than theirs, yet not once does He admit that He has in any degree fallen short of His own exacting standards.

At the end of His life, as He communed with His Father in His moving High Priestly Prayer, He claimed to have accomplished perfectly the work entrusted to Him (John 17:4). In any other case than His, we would be justified in regarding such claims as obnoxious pride and arrogant hypocrisy. In His case the facts substantiated the claim.

To quote T. C. Edwards again in this context, "The fact that Jesus never confessed sin implies in His case that He never did sin. In every other good man, the saintlier he becomes the more pitiless is his self-condemnation, and the more severe he is on certain kinds of sin, such as hypocrisy. But Jesus, if He were a sinner, was guilty of the very worst of sin, which He rebuked with burning anger in the Pharisees of His day. Yet He never accuses Himself. . . . He never speaks about redeeming Himself, but declares Himself to be the paschal lamb 'whose blood of the new covenant is shed for many unto the remission of sins'" (see Matthew 26:28).

While painting the doom of the impenitent in awful colors, He is quite unconcerned about His own salvation. He prayed, "Father, forgive them," but never, "Father, forgive Me."

It is a striking fact that the Scriptures that so faithfully record the sins and failures of their most notable heroes, such as Abraham and Moses and David, have no record of His sins or failures.

THE WITNESS OF FRIEND AND FOE

That Jesus was sinless appears to be the conviction of His contemporaries, whether friends or foes.

His disciples. For more than three years His disciples had daily opportunity to observe His actions and reactions under all possible circumstances. Had there been discrepancy between what He said and the way He lived, they would have been the first to observe and note it. But they consistently found in His life the embodiment of His teaching.

As honest men, had they detected any flaw or shortcoming, they would have recorded it as they did their own. But with one voice they exalt their Master as the perfect example of a holy life: "You disowned the Holy and Righteous One" (Acts 3:14). They openly declared of Him that He "committed no sin, and no deceit was found in his mouth" (1 Peter 2:22).

Judas. The testimony of Judas is of peculiar importance. After he had betrayed his best friend, he found he could not retain the wretched price of blood. Remorse compelled him to fling the silver at the feet of the chief priests and elders, saying, "I have betrayed innocent blood" (Matthew 27:4). So violent was the panic in his breast that he could bear life no longer, and "he went away and hanged himself." We may depend upon it that if Judas had ever seen, in public or in private, anything in the character of Jesus inconsistent with His claims, he would have dragged it into the light of day. But conscience compelled him to testify that He whom he betrayed was innocent. He was unable to extract a single crumb of comfort from any inconsistency in the life of Jesus.

The thief on the cross, deeply impressed by the words and demeanor of the Lord under the most agonizing conditions, gave as his testimony, "This man has done nothing wrong" (Luke 23:41).

The centurion, similarly impressed, could find no explanation for such serenity and triumph in the hour of suffering and death, except in the conviction that "surely he was the Son of God" (Matthew 27:54).

Both *Pilate and his wife* united to pronounce Him a just man (Matthew 27:19, 24).

Even *the demons* were forced to add their unwilling testimony, "I know who you are—the Holy One of God!" (Mark 1:24).

It should be borne in mind, however, that Jesus' perfection of character did not consist in merely *negative faultlessness.* Throughout His whole life He was characterized by positive and active holiness. There is no perfection of character of which we can conceive that does not find its ideal fulfillment in Him. The more closely His life is analyzed, the more completely His perfection shines out.

Throughout His earthly life, and through the succeeding centuries, hostile men have been searching for some flaw in His character, but in vain. One of the bitterest unbelievers was compelled in honesty to declare, "I wish to say once and for all, that to that great and serene man I pay, I gladly pay, the homage of my admiration and my tears."

COULD JESUS HAVE SINNED?

To attempt an answer to a question that has found strong champions ranged on either side in the limits of space available is an impossible task. Contenders for each viewpoint are agreed that Jesus *did not* sin. But *could* He have sinned? Some attribute to Christ the inability to sin, whereas others will concede only that He was able not to sin.

In advocating the latter view, Everett F. Harrison wrote: "To insist that Jesus could have sinned, takes the incident out of line with the original probation. By reducing the Temptation to a demonstration of sinlessness, the nerve connection is cut with believers also, for then it would be logically impossible for New Testament writers to appeal to Jesus' temptation as a ground of confidence for the believer's overcoming of temptation by His sympathetic help [Hebrews 2:18; 4:14–15]. . . . If we affirm the inability of the man Jesus to sin, we are affirming a qualitative difference between the humanity of the first Adam and that of the Last Adam."

For the former view, John Macleod contends: "Those who content themselves with ascribing only a *posse non peccare* of Him and refuse to acknowledge a *non posse peccare,* fail to maintain the unity of His Person,

93

while they acknowledge the distinction in Him of two natures, that of God and that of man."

We must admit that here we are in the realm of mystery, for there can never be, from the nature of the case, a simplistic explanation of the twofold nature of our Lord. But there are factors that must be given due weight.

On the one hand, to us the thought of temptation without the possibility of sinning seems unreal. But Scripture affirms that Jesus was tempted in all points as we are (Hebrews 4:15), yet never for a moment did He entertain succumbing to temptation.

On the other hand, consider the implications of the possibility of His being able to sin. He was the God-man—divine and human natures completely united in one personality—and if He could have sinned then God could sin, which is unthinkable.

It would seem that even according to His human nature He was unable to sin. How could "that holy being" that was conceived by the Holy Spirit be susceptible to sin? If it be asked that if this were so, how could Jesus have suffered in the temptation? we would reply that suffering is most poignant in those who do not sin, not in those who yield. The suffering of temptation lies in our resistance to it. Yielding to it means giving up the struggle.

Again, if Jesus could have sinned when on earth, He could sin now, for is He not "the same yesterday and today and forever" (Hebrews 13:8)? And would this not place the whole work of redemption on a very shaky foundation?

To this writer, despite the other problems involved, the thought that God could be implicated in sin of His own doing is intolerable. The final solution of the problem must be left until the day when hidden things are revealed.

The following paragraph by an unknown writer is a fitting close to this study.

In vain do we look through the entire biography of Jesus for a single stain, or the slightest shadow on His moral character. He injured nobody, He never spoke an improper word, He never committed a wrong action. Ingenious malignity looks in vain for the slightest trace of self-seeking in His motives; sensuality shrinks abashed from His celestial purity; falsehood can leave no stain on Him who is incarnate Truth; injustice is forgotten beside His errorless equity; the very possibility of avarice is swallowed up in His benignity and love; the very idea of ambition is lost in His divine wisdom and self-abnegation.

KEY INSIGHT
INTO THE LIFE AND WORK OF CHRIST

Christ never admitted to falling short to any degree of the high standards He taught, nor could anyone else find fault with Him.

14

THE TRANSFIGURATION OF CHRIST

This glorious event, which has been termed one of the most astonishing of all our Lord's experiences on earth, has received too little attention in contemporary teaching and preaching. The Transfiguration was the one occasion on which the full glory of the Godhead was permitted to blaze forth. F. F. Bruce expresses the feeling of many when he says that the Transfiguration is one of the passages in our Lord's earthly history that a Bible scholar would rather pass over in reverent silence, for who is able fully to speak of that wondrous night scene among the mountains, during which heaven was for a few brief moments brought down to earth, and the mortal body of Jesus shone with celestial brightness?

THE MOUNT OF TRANSFIGURATION

The location is almost certainly Mount Hermon and not Mount Tabor. Mark informs us that, after the event, Jesus "left that place and passed through Galilee" (Mark 9:30) to Capernaum, and thence to Jerusalem. An intermediate visit from Caesarea to Tabor and then twenty miles to Capernaum would seem to be purposeless. Further, at that time Tabor was crowned with a fortified city, which would render it unsuitable for such a manifestation. The incidental mention of the cloud that enveloped them corresponds with the rapid cloud formation characteristic of Mount Hermon. Since it is recorded that the disciples were heavy with sleep, a scene at night is probably described.

The memorable privilege of being present on this occasion was granted to only three disciples, our Lord's intimate disciples, Peter and James and John; intimate not because of favoritism, but because they more than the others were willing to pay the high price of following Him closely. Like them, we are each as close to the Lord as we really choose to be.

For those three it was an unforgettable experience. In reading John's record of it written half a century later, we can almost detect the awe in his words, "We have seen his glory, the glory of the One and Only, who came from the Father" (John 1:14). Peter too records the indelible impression the experience made on him: "We were eyewitnesses of his majesty" (2 Peter 1:16). The passing years had only served to deepen their awe and wonder.

SIGNIFICANCE TO CHRIST

This incident undoubtedly meant much to the "God-man" in the days of His humiliation. Following Peter's great and comforting confession of His deity, the voice of His Father again confirmed to Him His divine Sonship. He had shared with the disciples the fact of His impending death, and now two heavenly prophets, Moses and Elijah, converse with Him about His coming death. He had predicted that He would come again in glory, and now His disciples are given a foretaste of that glory.

In the absence of sympathy and spiritual dullness of His earthly friends, this interlude when He received fresh assurance of heaven's approval would be greatly treasured. It would assure them, too, that He was not speaking empty words when He told them He would rise from the dead and meet the saints of old in a state of glory. Such a blessed experience would do much to embolden and strengthen Him for the grim ordeal that lay ahead.

SIGNIFICANCE TO THE DISCIPLES

He was transfigured before His disciples (Mark 9:2). It was to them that the voice came from heaven, "This is my Son, whom I love; with him I am well pleased. Listen to him" (Matthew 17:5). To them the radiant sight must have held great significance, confirming the Lord's prediction of His impending death at Jerusalem. The vision of glory would reconcile them somewhat to His sufferings.

His essential deity was manifested before them in such a way as to dispel doubt. The purpose of His mission to earth was interpreted to them by the two chosen representatives of Judaism—Moses and Elijah. At last they were fully convinced of the preeminence of Christ, and the memory would help carry them over the coming days of gloom. The presence of Moses and Elijah would be the pledge of their own immortality. There was tangible evidence that the grave is not the end.

There was granted to these disciples a threefold vision.

A vision of His glory. "We have seen his glory" was John's comment. It appears as though the evangelists vie with each other in their attempt to convey the impression of the glory of the Lord on that occasion. Mark records that "his clothes became dazzling white, whiter than anyone in the world could bleach them" (Mark 9:3; see also Matthew 17:2). Luke adds other elements: "The appearance of his face changed, and his clothes became as bright as a flash of lightning" (Luke 9:29). The "form of God" shone through the form of a servant (Philippians 2:6 KJV).

These descriptions make clear that the illumination was not merely external, as from a spotlight. The change came from within, first the countenance and then the garments, which had the translucent whiteness of pure light. Common to all records are the two features of dazzling whiteness and blazing light. Combining the three descriptions, we have the purity of snow, the majesty of lightning, and the benign aspect of light emanating from the person of the Lord. Small wonder that Peter wanted the experience continued!

Wilbur Smith maintains that we are justified in saying that there was some actual physical change in our Lord's body—an actual change, not rays of light on His face and clothes. If it was, as would appear, a nocturnal scene, where would this bright light come from? The change they saw in His countenance was only the visible manifestation of a change that had taken place in His whole body. His garments shone from the emergence of the brilliant light coming from the transfigured body of the Lord—an emanation from the fountain of light within Him.

The glory on Moses' face was merely reflected glory, whereas that of Christ was from within. Is it without significance that it was "as He prayed" that the fashion of His countenance was altered (Luke 9:29 KJV)? Is that not still the method of transfiguration in our lives?

A vision of His cross. The central theme of conversation at this remarkable gathering is recorded: "They spoke about his departure, which he was about to bring to fulfillment at Jerusalem" (Luke 9:31).

In the temple at Ravenna, there is a mosaic of the sixth century, which represents in symbolic form the transfiguration of Christ. A jeweled cross, set in the midst of a circle of blue, studded with golden stars, is presented to the eye of the observer. In the midst of the scene appears the cross of Christ, while from the cloud close by a divine hand appears that points to the cross. In the mind of the artist, the cross was the center of the Transfiguration scene. To unregenerate man, the cross is an offense, but to the inhabitants of heaven, far from being a disgrace, it is a glory and honor.

It is natural to ask why Moses and Elijah were chosen for this sacred rendezvous rather than, say, Abraham and Ezekiel. Was it because they were the only two who had experienced a revelation from God in which He caused a manifestation of Himself to pass before them (Exodus 33:17–23; 1 Kings 19:9–13)? Was it because of the peculiar nature of their own "exodus" that they were chosen to speak with Him of His exodus?

In any case it was most fitting that Moses and Elijah, the acknowledged representatives of the law and the prophets, should come together with Jesus on the mount. These were the heavenly ambassadors, commissioned by the Father to converse with His Son concerning His "exodus." The two representatives of Judaism surrendered their seals of office to their Master and Lord.

As the disciples listened in to heaven's sacred conversation, they were led to look at the impending death of their Lord from the viewpoint of heaven rather than from that of the world. We too need a new vision of the centrality and crucial nature of the cross in God's program.

A vision of His coming. In recalling his impression of the mountain scene, Peter wrote, "We did not follow cleverly invented stories when we told you about the power and coming of our Lord Jesus Christ, but we were eyewitnesses of his majesty" (2 Peter 1:16). He saw in that momentous event a foreshadowing of His power and coming. Could there be, in miniature, a clearer picture of the outstanding features of His advent?

How will He come? As He appeared on the Transfiguration mount, "with power and great glory" (Matthew 24:30). "He is coming with the clouds" (Revelation 1:7). "[He] comes in his [own] glory" (Matthew 25:31).

Who will meet Him? Those of whom *Moses* was a representative, "The dead in Christ" (1 Thessalonians 4:16). "Them also which sleep in Jesus" (1 Thessalonians 4:14 KJV). And those of whom *Elijah* was a representative—those who are translated at His coming and never see death. "We who are still alive and are left will be caught up . . . so we will be with the Lord forever" (1 Thessalonians 4:17). Could this be the explanation of the cryptic words of Jesus that precede the account of the scene? "Some who are standing here will not taste death before they see the kingdom of God" (Luke 9:27). It was a momentary glimpse of the kingdom to be set up when Christ returns in power to reign.

Moses and Elijah departed. The heavenly voice was silent. The clouds dispersed. "When [the disciples] looked up, they saw no one *except Jesus*" (Matthew 17:8, italics added).

KEY INSIGHT
INTO THE LIFE AND WORK OF CHRIST

In His transfiguration, the deity of Christ is revealed as fully as is humanly possible, as well as His mission on earth to conquer death.

15

THE PROPHETIC
MINISTRY OF CHRIST

Jesus was the crown of Old Testament prophecy. He was Himself the
perfect prophet, for in Him all the moral precepts and ritual laws con-
verged and united.

Among the Jews there was an eager expectation that a great prophet,
as massive and commanding in personality as Moses himself, would be
raised up by God in their nation. For this they had a scriptural basis: "The
LORD your God will raise up for you a prophet like me," Moses had
said (Deuteronomy 18:15). The priests and Levites cherished this hope,
hence their question to John the Baptist, who was moving the nation
by his flaming speeches: "Are you the Prophet?" (John 1:21). Peter also
referred to the promise in his address in the temple (Acts 3:22).

Later, when Jesus returned from the wilderness in the power of the
Spirit, "the whole city was stirred and asked, 'Who is this?' The crowds
answered, 'This is Jesus, the prophet from Nazareth'" (Matthew 21:10–11).
Further, Jesus called Himself a prophet.

THE PROPHETIC OFFICE

It is incorrect to think of the prophetic office as exclusively future
related. In the Bible sense, the word *prophecy* is not so limited. When

the woman of Samaria called Jesus a prophet, she did so not because He predicted the future but because He told her what she had done (John 4:19, 29). Daniel fulfilled the prophetic office as completely when he interpreted Nebuchadnezzar's dream as when he foretold the course of Gentile world supremacy.

Included in the prophetic role was the task of revealing and interpreting the will of God to mankind through the inspiration of the Holy Spirit, since the prophet was the medium of communication between God and men. In the words of Henry DeVries, "The chief function of the prophet is to receive the thoughts of God in his human consciousness, in order to impart the same to the people. Hence the Son of God, in order to be our prophet, must first of all assume our human consciousness, i.e., become man; for thus alone can He receive and impart the divine thoughts to us."

There are two elements in the ministry of the prophet: the passive function of receiving revelations of the divine will, and the active function of passing those on to the people. That may be done either in word or in symbolical prophetic actions, as demonstrated by Ezekiel. The functions are better described as insight and foresight.

In Old Testament times the prophet acted as the conscience of the nation, as a study of the prophetic books will demonstrate. They spoke out against the religious abuses of their day. They urged obedience to the divine law and warned of coming judgment in no uncertain terms.

The marks of the true prophet were that he had his message direct from God; that he was indifferent as to its acceptability or otherwise; and that he disregarded the consequences of delivering it, so far as his own welfare and comfort were concerned.

The prophets were "but instruments wholly dependent on Him who employed them. They were the voice, but not the speaker; the message, but not the sender; the musical instruments, but not the player."

CHRIST'S PROPHETIC MINISTRY

At His baptism in Jordan our Lord received the prophetic anointing, and it was there His prophetic ministry began (Matthew 4:23–25).

As prophet, He proclaimed the dawning of the kingdom of God, and with apocalyptic vision, He foretold its course.

As to the nature of His ministry, *it was predictive.* An essential element in the equipment of a prophet was that he should be able to see things in advance, should possess superhuman knowledge, the ability to see the end from the beginning.

Twice our Lord repeated the statement "I have told you now before it happens, so that when it does happen you will believe" (John 14:29; cf. 13:19). This ability to predict manifested itself in small matters as well as great, as, for example, His foresight in sending Peter to catch the fish and obtain the tribute money (Matthew 17:27). Or in His sending the disciples to bring the donkey on which He would ride into Jerusalem (Matthew 21:1–3).

Again, He foretold in detail the destruction of Jerusalem (Matthew 24:3–28) and of the temple (Mark 13:2). He outlined the whole course of this age and the worldwide sweep of gospel witness in the remarkable chapters about the end times, Matthew 24 and 25. To Him the future was an open book. No eventuality surprised Him. The cross and its attendant circumstances did not take Him unawares; He saw in advance the whole path to the cross.

It was authoritative. In none of His predictive statements did our Lord use the familiar prophetic formula used by all His predecessors, "Thus saith the Lord" or "The word of the Lord came unto me, saying," but instead He employed the authoritative "I say unto you." The word of the Lord did not come to Him; He was Himself the Word.

Those to whom Jesus preached recognized early the prophetic element in His words. "When Jesus had finished saying these things, the crowds were amazed at his teaching, because he taught as one who had authority, and not as their teachers of the law" (Matthew 7:28–29). And why? Because, as He claimed, His words were not His own but were drawn from the fountainhead of all wisdom—the Father.

In commenting on the element of authority in Christ's teaching, W. B. Riley noted: *(a)* His speech was without hesitation. *(b)* His statements were without qualification—He never employed language susceptible to different meanings with an intent to deceive His hearers. *(c)* His affirmations involved finality. His "I say unto you" closed the discussion. There was no higher authority to whom appeal could be made than to the greatest prophet Himself. His word was the end of controversy. *(d)* He neither needed nor consulted counselors. *(e)* His declarations amounted to commands.

It was interpretative. He was first and foremost the revealer and interpreter of divine truth. "The only begotten Son, which is in the bosom of the Father, he hath declared him" (John 1:18 KJV). He spoke of and for God, revealing the Father not only by His sinless life but mainly in His death (John 8:26; 14:9; 17:8).

It was confirmed. One method of fulfilling the prophetic office was the working of miracles. His mighty works authenticated His wonderful message (Matthew 8–9). Most of His miracles were in the realm of healing diseases and infirmity. Sickness is contagious with us. But Christ was an example of perfect health, and His health was contagious. By its overflow He healed others. Only a touch was necessary.

It is being continued. Another aspect of Christ's prophetic ministry is seen in His making the apostles infallible in the transmission of the truth recorded in the writings of the New Testament. If "the testimony of Jesus is the spirit of prophecy" (Revelation 19:10), then all the apostles' writings affirm that what they teach is received from Jesus through His Spirit.

His prophetic office is being continued as He mediates through the gifts of ministry in the church in conjunction with the inspired Word (John 16:12–14; Acts 1:1). The church is a prophetic institution whose function it is to teach the world by its preaching and ordinances. The faithful ministers of the Word today are the successors of the prophets and continue the work of the great prophet who surpassed every grace and gift distributed through those who preach Him.

"To complete the magnificence of the prophetic office," wrote Harry Rimmer, "the work of Jesus will end with the final and complete revelation of the Father to His saints in glory. When the Body of Christ is completed by the regeneration of the last one who is to be saved by faith, the trump shall sound, the dead in Christ shall rise, and the living saints translated to meet Christ in the air. In that form He shall Himself present His Church to His Father, and shall present His Father unveiled to His Church so that we see God and know Him as He is. Magnificent, indeed is that Prophet who can fulfill all prophecy and bring God within the sphere of human comprehension."

KEY INSIGHT
INTO THE LIFE AND WORK OF CHRIST

Christ spoke with authority, predicting and interpreting future events and then confirming them with His works.

16

THE TEACHING
OF CHRIST

W e know you are a teacher who has come from God," said Nicodemus on his nocturnal visit to Jesus (John 3:2). "No one ever
spoke the way this man does," averred the officers of the chief priests who
were sent to apprehend Him (John 7:46).

It is widely conceded that Jesus is the peerless teacher of the ages. True,
He lived in an age when many outstanding teachers had exercised far-
reaching influence, but He towers above them all in solitary splendor.

Sir Edward Arnold, one of the greatest authorities on Buddhism, declared that one sentence from the Sermon on the Mount was worth more
than everything Buddha had ever taught.

"What sweetness," exclaimed the unbeliever Rousseau, "what purity
is found in the attitudes of Christ! What an affecting gracefulness in His
instructions! What wisdom in His teachings!"

Forty-five times the Gospels refer to Jesus as teacher, and a great
part of His time was occupied with teaching one or two or three or
twelve disciples. He called Himself by the same name. "You call me
'Teacher' and 'Lord,' and rightly so, for that is what I am" (John 13:13).
His followers were therefore called disciples, or learners.

We shall look first at the manner and then at the matter of His
teaching.

THE MANNER OF HIS TEACHING

It was dogmatic. His favorite formula, "Verily, verily, I say unto thee" (John 3:3 KJV), left no room for argument. Those who heard Him teach were amazed at the contrast between Him and the scribes, "because he taught as one who had authority" (Matthew 7:29). Unlike them, He did not have to refer to the teachings of others. His was an authoritative word. "Moses said . . . but I say unto you . . ."

It has been well said that His authority was not the charisma of a great reputation but the irresistible force of a divine message delivered under a sense of divine mission.

When Jesus spoke on any subject, there was nothing more that needed to be said. The Jewish leaders could not but recognize this quality, repugnant though it was to them. Even though they were not prepared to recognize His messiahship, they were ready to acknowledge His unique gifts as teacher.

It was simple. No other teacher has so skillfully and successfully combined simplicity and profundity. In His sayings there is an absence of too much scholarship or striving for an effect. No one in His audience ever needed to scratch his head and wonder what the preacher was aiming at, even though he may not have understood the full spiritual significance of the words. "His illustrations are commonplace, His words within the reach of the humblest. Are they real in faith and honest in heart? Then the poorest are capable of recognizing His simple teaching, and following it as in His perfect life," wrote Horace Bushnell.

Our Lord thought in images, and His teaching was full of figures of speech. His parables—concise and pointed stories in figurative style—expressed spiritual truths so vividly and lucidly that they have affected the lives of all generations. How could He more effectively have portrayed His Father's love than in the parable of the prodigal son? The words of Jesus had an incomparable directness that left a clear and indelible impression on His hearers.

Although Jesus did not contradict the findings of true science or other disciplines in anything He said, He made no overt references to them. There is an absence of technical terms and a minimum of theological expressions in His teaching. Small wonder that "the common people heard him gladly" (Mark 12:37 KJV).

It was vital. Our Lord never wasted time on secondary topics but always dealt with the fundamentals in people's thinking. The speculative and theoretical found scant place in His teaching. He always went right to the heart of things. All He said and taught revolved around the plan of salvation in one or another of its aspects. He never said anything shallow or trivial.

It was ethical. He impressed on His hearers that doctrine was valueless unless transformed into holy living. It was not sufficient for men to "talk the walk." They must "walk the talk." His Sermon on the Mount is the loftiest ethical pronouncement of all time. He did not scale down His ethical demands to meet the limitations of sinful human nature.

It was practical. No sermon Jesus preached lacked personal application. Nor was His method always to reserve the application until the end. When the sermon began, the application followed. No member of His audience was left in doubt as to the person to whom it applied. They were either enraptured or enraged, but they could not remain neutral.

G. K. Chesterton maintained that it could never be said that the teaching of Christ had been tried and found wanting. It has only been found difficult and not tried.

It was psychologically correct. The maker of the human mind knew best how to approach it, and here a wealth of wisdom in dealing with the spiritual problems of individuals opens up to us. To analyze the sermons and conversations of the perfect teacher is to learn the ideal method of presenting truth. The psychologist must look up to Him with respect, for there has never been a man who knew men as He did; no one ever estimated human nature so fairly or could read the human soul so easily and perfectly. We have only to think of the masterly description of the human heart in the parable of the different kinds of ground (Matthew 13:3–19). "He knew what was in a man" (John 2:25).

It was original, but not in the sense of absolute newness, for much that Jesus said had parallels in Jewish and other literature. What He said was original in its manner of design, in its spirit and style. It was free from the clichés and deceptive logic of the Jewish teachings. Old truths were stated in new ways that challenged fresh thought and action. His teaching carries its own inner stamp of genuineness. It was original because His ideals and standards of greatness on many things were the very opposite of generally accepted standards.

AN EXAMPLE

James H. McConkey, who himself was remarkable for the particular clarity of his teaching of biblical truth, pointed out that there was a three-fold method in our Lord's flawless teaching. Taking Matthew 6:25–34 as an example, he indicated the three steps.

State. In this paragraph, Jesus is warning against the peril of anxious care. First He states the great truth He is about to teach. The value of crystal-clear statement of truth cannot be overestimated. To state the truths of the text lucidly will not only clarify it to the hearers but will be an excellent mental discipline for the teacher. That lawyer is most likely to win his case who can state it most lucidly to the jurors.

Illustrate. Next, Jesus followed up His statement with three exceedingly familiar yet effective illustrations—the birds of the air, the cubit of stature, the lilies of the field. Each illustration throws a beam of light on the truth He is seeking to enforce.

Our Lord's method here demonstrates the importance of the association of ideas, of linking the unknown with the known. The sky, the sea, the pearls, the sheep, and the well are all known. Profound though it was, a child could follow His teaching and profit by it. His illustrations were not only simple, but they were familiar to the people to whom they were spoken.

Apply. There is no point in mixing a cold remedy unless you take it. There is little use in stating truths and illustrating them if the truth is not applied to the heart and conscience of the listener. Jesus searchingly applied His teaching on worry and anxiety. He did not fear to make it pointedly personal. He used personal pronouns, "you," "ye." He did not avoid repetition to reinforce His lesson.

THE MATTER OF HIS TEACHING

It is of interest to note the dominant themes in the teaching of the Lord and to test our own teaching by His standards. It is noteworthy that He did not propose any special system of doctrine, nor did He adopt the current theological jargon, but spoke the language of daily life. He dealt with deep and enduring principles and overarching truths of perpetual relevance.

Among the prominent themes in His teaching are these.

The *kingdom of God,* or the *kingdom of heaven.* These expressions collectively occur some seventy-eight times and represent thirty different occasions in His ministry. The terms have a *universal* application in the sense that God is "King" with reference to the universe or any part of the entire creation. They have a *spiritual* significance and refer to the messianic reign in the heart and life of the believer. A great many of Jesus' parables are concerned with the nature, growth, and consummation of the kingdom.

Eternal life is a theme especially prominent in John's writings and vitally related to the kingdom of God. In Christ's teaching we are in the presence of abiding and eternal life.

Sin and righteousness are everywhere in evidence. The reality and destructiveness of sin and the necessity and availability of righteousness form a background to His teaching.

His death and resurrection occupy a disproportionate part of the gospel records. Although His disciples were slow to discern the full significance of His words, Jesus sought to show them His coming death in its divine perspective.

God the Father. Since He had come to reveal the Father, this truth inevitably crops up constantly in His teachings. But His presentation of the Fatherhood of God made it abundantly clear that only those who were united to Him by faith were included in its scope.

The Holy Spirit. As the time for His departure from the earth drew near, the mission and ministry of the Comforter assumed increasing prominence in His conversation with His disciples.

The life to come. He did not leave men to grope around in the mists of uncertainty, but gave clear instructions concerning what lay beyond the veil.

In recounting his return pilgrimage from unbelief to faith, G. J. Romanes said that one thing that especially impressed him was that in contrast with the words of other world teachers, even Plato, the words of Jesus do not become obsolete with the lapse of time. They do not grow old. He confessed that he did not know any part of Christ's teaching that the subsequent growth of human knowledge has proven false.

Jesus will forever remain the peerless preacher. The Christian pulpit has not produced His equal in the art of giving truth to men through the spoken word. Jesus of Nazareth abides without a rival as the world's master teacher.

KEY INSIGHT
INTO THE LIFE AND WORK OF CHRIST

> *Jesus made clear that doctrine was not of value unless it is combined with holy living, so He often illustrated His points and provided application.*

17

THE HUMILITY
OF CHRIST

In the words "I am *meek* and *lowly* in heart" (Matthew 11:29 KJV, italics added), Jesus gave us a glimpse into His innermost heart. If pride is the greatest and central sin, then humility is the supreme virtue; and if humility was the distinguishing feature of the Master, then it must characterize the disciple, for "the servant is not greater than his lord" (John 13:16 KJV).

Had Jesus never spoken a word about humility, His daily life and circumstances would have been a constant unspoken rebuke to the pride and self-exaltation of the men and women with whom He associated. He was not only a standing rebuke to pride but a living example of humility.

In his *Modern Painters,* John Ruskin identifies true humility: "I believe the first test of a truly great man is his humility. I do not mean by humility doubt of his own power, or hesitation in speaking his own opinions, but a right understanding of the relation between what he can do, and the rest of the world's sayings and doings. All great men not only know their business, but usually know that they know it, and are not only right in their main opinions, but they usually know that they are right in them, only they do not think much of themselves on that account. Arnolfo knows that he can build a great dome at Florence; Albert Durer writes calmly to one who has found fault with his work, 'It cannot be done better'; Sir Isaac Newton knows that he has worked out a problem or two that would have puzzled anyone else; only they do not expect their fellow men therefore to fall down and worship them."

A DESPISED GRACE

The works of the great philosophers of past days do not contain the exaltation of humility as a virtue. In vain will their lives, too, be examined for evidence of true Christian humility. The reverse is the case. There is no word in either Greek or Latin that expresses the Christian idea of humility. The word "lowly" (KJV; "humble," NIV) which Jesus appropriated to Himself, is employed by ethical philosophers such as Socrates, Plato, and Xenophon in a derogatory sense. Even Josephus, the Hebrew historian and moralist, invested the word with a similar meaning. "Humility is a vice with the heathen moralists," said J. B. Lightfoot.

Not until Jesus came with His peerless life and matchless teaching was humility elevated to the level of a primary virtue. Humility as a grace is the creation of Christianity. Since the Greeks used the word generally as signifying base or mean-spirited, it is readily understood that our Lord's pronouncements on the subject introduced His disciples to a startlingly new and revolutionary scale of values. "Whoever humbles himself will be exalted" (Matthew 23:12). "He who is least among you all— he is the greatest" (Luke 9:48). It was a difficult lesson for them to master, that humility was to be desired, not despised.

Meekness plus lowliness equals humility. Meekness is humility in relation to God. Lowliness is humility in relation to man. It is possible to be meek and not lowly. Jesus was just as meek toward God as He was lowly before man.

In common usage, meekness is almost synonymous with weakness, or an inferiority complex, and is usually attributed to those who are negative or insignificant. Yet has our divine Lord not crowned this modest character quality as queen of virtues? Otto Borchert contrasts the genuine humility of the Lord, which manifested itself in the utter absence of any striving after magnification or originality, with Muhammad, who was always sensitive to his personal appearance. The vanity of Buddha peeps through the rags of his beggar's cloak. But Jesus moved about in the unaffected guise of ordinary folk. "He humbled himself" (Philippians 2:13).

This otherworldly humility was seen most clearly in His giving up the outward appearance of His deity and taking His place in humanity, and then giving up even His place in humanity! This was humility indeed.

Think of His attitude *toward worldly position:* "Isn't this the carpenter's son?" (Matthew 13:55). *Toward earthly riches:* "For your sakes he became poor" (2 Corinthians 8:9). *Toward service:* "I am among you as one who serves" (Luke 22:27). *Toward suffering:* "I have a baptism to undergo, and how distressed I am until it is completed!" (Luke 12:50).

The completeness with which Jesus laid aside the independent exercise of His divine attributes and subordinated Himself to His Father is seen in the following passages: "I seek not mine own will" (John 5:30 KJV). "I seek not mine own glory" (John 8:50 KJV). "My teaching is not my own" (John 7:16). "The Son can do nothing by himself" (John 5:19). "I am not here on my own" (John 7:28). "These words you hear are not my own" (John 14:24). "I do nothing on my own" (John 8:28). Christ was willing to be nothing, in order that His Father might be all.

Jesus' humility was so absolute that His Father was able to achieve His whole will through Him. Because He so humbled Himself, "God exalted him to the highest place" (Philippians 2:9). Because His humility was the expression of His innermost attitude and not a temporary posture, He unassumingly donned the slave's apron and moved in and out among men as the servant of all. He drew attention to neither His achievements nor His humility.

Nowhere was His humility more strikingly displayed than in the way in which He bore insult and injury. During His brief years of ministry almost every form of trial assailed Him. A dozen times plots were laid against His life. What would be the attitude of a modern dictator to a would-be assassin? They said He was demon-possessed. They said He was mad. They slandered Him as a glutton and a drunkard. They attacked His motives and cast aspersions on His character. But all those combined failed to elicit one drop of bitterness or draw forth one word of complaint or self-justification from His lips. "As a sheep before her shearers is silent, so he did not open his mouth" (Isaiah 53:7).

HE TOOK A TOWEL

There are only two places in Scripture where it is explicitly stated that our Lord left us an example, and one of them was an example of unparalleled humility.

The disciples had gone to a room where the Last Supper had been prepared. On the way, the ambitious disciples had been quarreling over who should be the greatest and who would have precedence in Christ's kingdom. When they entered the room, there was apparently no slave to perform the customary washing of the feet of the guests. The disciples probably took turns when there was no slave, but on this occasion none would condescend to do the menial task. Their minds were full of the subject of their bitter contention, and none was willing to be servant of all. Each feigned unconsciousness of the neglected duty.

When Jesus entered, He found them seated in sulky silence, and supper must have been a gloomy meal. The scene that followed is described in moving words: "And supper being ended . . . Jesus knowing . . . that he was come from God, and went to God; he riseth from supper, and laid aside his garments; and took a towel, and girded himself . . . and began to wash the disciples' feet, and to wipe them with the towel" (John 13:2–5 KJV).

The quality of this act of humility is heightened by the fact that Jesus performed it while vividly conscious of His divine origin and nature. He knew that He came from God's presence. None of the disciples would confess himself inferior to another, but when the divine Lord remembered who He was, He rose up and performed the lowliest of tasks. And it was no act of ostentation; He did it just because He liked to do this for His disciples. On the other hand, we should not overlook the fact that when people fell in worship at His feet, Jesus did not bid them stand up. He accepted their worship as His due (Luke 7:38).

THE HUMILITY OF CHRIST

JESUS' TEACHING ON HUMILITY

A selection of Scripture passages will reveal the high place our Lord accorded to this grace.

"Blessed are the poor in spirit" (Matthew 5:3).

"Blessed are the meek" (Matthew 5:5).

"Whoever humbles himself like this little child is the greatest in the kingdom of heaven" (Matthew 18:4).

"He who humbles himself will be exalted" (Luke 14:11).

"The greatest among you should be like the youngest, and the one who rules like the one who serves" (Luke 22:26).

"I am among you as one who serves" (Luke 22:27).

"Learn from me, for I am gentle and humble in heart" (Matthew 11:29).

"He who is least among you all—he is the greatest" (Luke 9:48).

To read these passages thoughtfully is to be convicted of our own lack of humility. Our pride stands abashed in the presence of His utter humility. One fact stands out crystal clear—*God's way up is down.*

Andrew Murray indicates the way in which our Lord's humility may become ours: "It is only by the indwelling of Christ in His divine humility that we become truly humble. We have our pride from another, from Adam; we must have our humility from Another too. Pride is ours, and rules us with such terrible power, because it is our self, our very nature. Humility must be ours in the same way; it must be in our very self, our very nature. The promise is, 'where,' even in the heart, 'sin abounded, grace did abound more exceedingly.'"

KEY INSIGHT
INTO THE LIFE AND WORK OF CHRIST

*The paradox of Christ's humility
is that although He completely
accepted the worship of His disciples,
at the same time He could become
like a servant and wash their feet.*

18

THE SERENITY
OF CHRIST

W hen they had sung a hymn, they went out to the Mount of Olives"
(Matthew 26:30). This precious fragment is preserved for us by
both Matthew and Mark. Otherwise we should not have known that
the Savior sang under the very shadow of the cross. What serenity and
inward triumph is reflected in this revealing sentence! The Son of God
approaches the sorrows of Gethsemane and the sufferings of Golgotha
with a song on His lips. Anyone can sing in the sunshine, but to sing in
the darkness is a rare accomplishment.

And a sweet song it must have been. "Providence has veiled from us
any view of the physical characteristics of our Savior," wrote M. E. Dodd.
"There is divine wisdom in this. There is one expression in the Book
of Revelation, however, which refers to the voice of 'Him who was, and
is, and is to be,' as 'the sound of many waters.' If this is meant to be in
any particular a literal description of His voice, it means that His voice
was marvellous beyond anything that ever came from a human."

Jesus had eagerly anticipated this Last Supper with His disciples. "I
have eagerly desired to eat this Passover with you before I suffer," He
said to them (Luke 22:15). Gathered around the festal meal, they together
recalled the first Passover, when God liberated Israel from the hand of
Pharaoh, passing over them and protecting them from the judgment

that befell Egypt. The poignant realization that the sacrifice of the paschal lamb would so soon find fulfillment in His death would sweep over Him. So now He transforms the Passover Feast into the Lord's Supper, a sacrament that will be observed throughout the world by people of every nation and in every age as a memorial of His undying love.

The weak little group whom He was so soon to leave as helpless sheep in the midst of ravenous wolves drew out His deepest compassion. How tender were His words in those closing hours of fellowship, marred though they had been through their carnal rivalry and jostling for positions of power. His washing of the disciples' feet was no theatrical display but simply the spontaneous expression of a humble and loving heart.

Before they left the Passover table, it was the custom to sing a hymn, and what a thrilling male chorus they must have made, with Jesus Himself as the leader. Amazingly enough, we know the very hymn they sang, if not the melody.

At the feasts of Passover, Pentecost, Dedication, and Tabernacles, part of the ritual was the singing of Psalms 113–118, originally one song, and not divided into psalms. Together, those psalms were known as "the Hallel," a term meaning "to praise." It was the practice to divide the group of hymns into two parts, one of which was repeated in the middle of the banquet, the other reserved until the end.

So the hymn they sang following the pouring of the fourth cup consisted of Psalms 115–118. But what the Jews sang with blinded eyes, Jesus sang with clear vision. He discerned the inner meaning of Old Testament prophecy. Since He was leader of the feast, it would be up to Him to start the tune. It is not difficult to imagine the beautiful tones, full of feeling, with which He would sing some of those words, if we read the psalms thoughtfully and try to enter into His emotions as He sang them for the last time.

THE CHIEF CORNERSTONE

One of the richest verses of the hymn is Psalm 118:22: "The stone the builders rejected has become the capstone."

In the construction of Solomon's temple, "they brought great stones, costly stones, and hewed stones, to lay the foundation of the house" (1 Kings 5:17 KJV). A Jewish tradition records that one of the shaped stones was of odd design and size and did not seem to fit anywhere. So the masons discarded it, pushing it over into the valley of the Kidron. As the temple neared completion, it was found that the chief cornerstone was missing. A message was dispatched to the quarries to bring it up. Back came the answer that they had sent it up long before. Diligent search proved unavailing, until one of the masons remembered the stone that had been rejected as useless. With much effort it was drawn up from the valley and was found to fit exactly into place.

In the last week of His ministry our Lord exclaimed to the hostile chief priests and elders, "Have you never read in the Scriptures: 'The stone the builders rejected has become the capstone'?" (Matthew 21:42). He had experienced to the full the rejection of His nation, for when He came to His own home, His people had rejected Him (John 1:11).

But as He sang these same words with His disciples (Psalm 118:22), His heart pulsed with joy when He foresaw the day now so near when He who did not fit into man's temple at His first coming would become the Head of the corner at His second advent. This was doubtless part of "the joy set before him" (Hebrews 12:2), which enabled Him to endure the cross and despise its shame.

THIS IS THE DAY

Another verse of the hymn would challenge His acceptance of His Father's will: "This is the day the LORD has made; let us rejoice and be glad in it" (Psalm 118:24). That Jehovah had made "this day," the day of His cross, He knew, for had it not been preceded by an eternity of anticipation? And had it not been foretold in unmistakable terms?

But how could He rejoice in it when He knew it held shame, rejection, reproach, anguish? The answer is that in eternity, as in time, He always found joy in doing His Father's will, whatever the cost to Himself. "I delight to do thy will, O my God" (Psalm 40:8 KJV; see also

Hebrews 10:7). He found the joy of doing His Father's will so utterly satisfying that, with clear knowledge of what lay ahead, He was able to sing with insight, "This is the day the Lord has made; [I] will be glad and rejoice in it." Although He knew that in a few hours His Father's face would be averted from Him because of His identification with the sin of a world of men, He still sang, "Give thanks to the LORD, for he is good; his love endures forever" (Psalm 118:29).

"BLESSED IS HE WHO COMES"

Not many days before, a remarkable demonstration had taken place when Jesus entered Jerusalem sitting on a donkey. "A very large crowd spread their cloaks on the road, while others cut branches from the trees and spread them on the road. The crowds that went ahead of him and those that followed shouted, 'Hosanna to the Son of David! *Blessed is he who comes in the name of the Lord!* Hosanna in the highest!' When Jesus entered Jerusalem, the whole city was stirred and asked, 'Who is this?' The crowds answered, 'This is Jesus, the prophet from Nazareth in Galilee'" (Matthew 21:8–11, italics added).

As He sang these words, He was anticipating that in a few hours the adulation of the crowd would turn into the sullen roar "Crucify Him!" Even that did not quench His song.

But not only did He go to the cross with a song on His lips, but the last words of the song were words of thanksgiving: "Give thanks to the LORD, for he is good; his love endures forever" (Psalm 118:29). With these words, amid the shadows cast by the Passover moon, He led the little band to the olive garden.

What can we learn from the Passover song? We learn that we can turn our trouble into treasure and our sorrow into song. We can sing the song of faith in the darkest hour. Sorrow and singing are not incompatible.

KEY INSIGHT
INTO THE LIFE AND WORK OF CHRIST

Though He faced a painful crucifixion, Jesus sang hymns of hope and trust, completely calm in the knowledge of the great victory that was coming.

19

THE PRAYER LIFE
OF CHRIST

A ll of us tend to think that the human needs of our Lord were not as real or as pressing as our own. We feel that in some way His humanity was supported by His divine nature. But did His deity lessen the anguish of the Garden of Gethsemane or of the cross? Did it eliminate His hunger or weariness? Though He was truly divine, His deity in no way affected the reality of His human nature. His prayers were as sincere and intense as any ever offered.

His prayer life bore eloquent testimony to this. He completely renounced the independent exercise of His divine powers and privileges. He became like the weakest of His followers, dependent on His Father for everything. He received His daily and hourly needs through the medium of prayer, as we do.

Let us learn of Him from the gospel records.

HIS POSTURE IN PRAYER

Although bodily posture is secondary to the attitude of the soul, it is instructive to note that at times Jesus prayed while *standing,* wherever He happened to be at the moment (Matthew 14:19). At another time, He *knelt* (Luke 22:41), while on yet another occasion it is recorded that

He *fell on His face* (Matthew 26:39). If the Son of God got down upon His knees, yes, upon His face before God, what attitude should we ordinary mortals assume as we go into His presence?

Posture is not everything, but it does show reverence.

THE PLACE OF HIS PRAYERS

Much of the prayer life of Jesus was concealed, even from His intimate friends, but enough is recorded to stimulate both interest and imitation.

He prayed in secret. His own practice was reflected in His command to His disciples to engage in private prayer behind closed doors (Matthew 6:6)—shut in with God, shut out from everything else. Secret prayer always brings the open reward.

He prayed in company with others. Jesus frequently took some of His disciples away for prayer. His instruction in this discipline, both by precept and example, kindled in their hearts such a longing to master it themselves, that they asked Him, "Lord, teach us to pray" (Luke 11:1). His longest public prayer was offered in the presence of His disciples (John 17).

He prayed in solitude on the mountainside. The majesty and solitude of the mountainside created a subtle fascination for Him. James Stalker suggested that when Jesus reached a new town, He first thought of the shortest way to the mountain, just as travelers ask the way to the best hotel.

Jesus enjoyed a solitude not of time and place only but a solitude of spirit that is much more difficult to attain. Consider the paradoxical statement "Once when Jesus was praying in private and his disciples were with him" (Luke 9:18). He apparently possessed such powers of concentration that even their presence did not disturb the solitude of His spirit.

THE OCCASIONS OF HIS PRAYERS

Luke records nine occasions when Jesus prayed: at His baptism (Luke 3:21), after a day of miracles (Luke 5:15–16), before choosing His disciples (Luke 6:12), before the first prediction of His death (Luke 9:18), on the Mount of Transfiguration (Luke 9:29), before teaching the disciples to pray (Luke 11:1), when the seventy returned with their report (Luke 10:21), in the Garden of Gethsemane (Luke 22:39–46), and on the cross (Luke 23:34, 46).

A study of these occasions in His life that led to prayer will provide much instruction for our own prayer lives.

He prayed *in the morning,* at the beginning of the day (Mark 1:35), and *in the evening,* when the day's work was over (Mark 6:46).

Great crises came after prayer. It was while He prayed that the Holy Spirit descended on Him and the silence of heaven was broken by the Father's sign of His divine Sonship (Luke 3:21–22). His selection of His twelve disciples—a seemingly insignificant event, yet crucial in church history—was made only after He had spent a night in prayer (Luke 6:12–13). They were to be not only His companions but also the messengers of His teaching after He had gone. It was after a special time of prayer that He unburdened His heart to them concerning His impending suffering and death (Luke 9:18, 21–22). The Transfiguration was an answer to His prayer (Luke 9:28–36). Prayer was the cause, the Transfiguration the effect.

Great achievements came after prayer. His feeding of the four thousand (Matthew 15:36) and the five thousand (John 6:11), walking on water (Matthew 14:23–33), raising of Lazarus (John 11:41–42), and healing the insane boy (Mark 9:14–29) were each the outcome of prayer.

Great achievements were also followed by prayer. When confronted with great crises or with demanding tasks, we instinctively turn to prayer. But once the crisis is past and the task achieved, the tendency is to once again lean on our own ability or wisdom. Jesus guarded against that tendency by following up such occasions with prayer. After what had been perhaps one of the most successful days of His whole ministry, it is recorded that, instead of courting popularity, He sent the crowd away and departed to a mountain to pray (Matthew 14:23). We would be well advised to follow our divine Master in this habit.

Great pressure of work was a call to extra prayer. Our Lord's life was exceptionally busy. He worked under constant pressure. At times He had no leisure even for meals, but the pressure of the crowds was never permitted to crowd out prayer. We are apt to use the pressure of our work as a reason for *not* praying. With Jesus, it was a reason for giving extra time to prayer (see Luke 5:15–16; Mark 1:35; Luke 4:42; John 6:15).

Great sorrows were confronted in prayer. As the Man of Sorrows, He suffered deeply through the crass materialism of His own people and the tragic lack of understanding on the part of His own disciples. But the greatest sorrow of all was to be the "bruising" and "forsaking" by His Father. He fortified Himself by prayer for that (Matthew 26:36–46; John 6:15; 11:41–42; 12:28).

He died praying. The habit of a lifetime cannot be quenched even in the hour of death. His last utterance was one of trustful prayer (Luke 23:46).

THE CHARACTER OF HIS PRAYERS

It is true that only small fragments of the Master's life are preserved for us in the Gospels, but a large field may be seen through a small opening in the fence. The prayers of His that are recorded give us a rich insight into His character as well as material for our imitation.

His prayers revealed His role as a Son. Observe how He addresses God in His prayers in the Upper Room and in Gethsemane. "Father." "O my Father" (KJV). "My Father." "Holy Father." The sense of His own Sonship and of God's Fatherhood formed the background of His prayer life. The glory of His Father was His consuming passion (John 17:4).

His prayers were filled with thanksgiving. Adoring thankfulness constantly welled up in His grateful heart. "I thank thee, O Father" was a characteristic expression in His prayers (Matthew 11:25; Luke 10:21, both KJV). Whether He walked in the light or in the shadow of difficulties, thanksgiving was an important part of His life.

His prayers included no confession of sin. There was never any consciousness of disobedience or sense of distance from His Father in His heart. He not only "committed no sin" (1 Peter 2:22) but positively asserted, "I always do what pleases him" (John 8:29). No occasion for confession ever arose.

In His prayer, communion with the Father played a large role. It would seem that in true prayer, petition for personal needs occupies only a secondary place. Jesus missed the glory and communion He had shared with the Father (John 17:5), and after living in the foul sin-filled air of earth He longed for the clear atmosphere of heaven. His High Priestly Prayer is a choice example of communion with God at its highest.

His prayers included petition and supplication—prayer for His own needs and those of His friends and followers. His intercessions included the interests and spiritual advancement of His disciples (Luke 22:32), the deep need of those who had not experienced His saving grace, the rebellious, and even those who crucified Him (Luke 23:34). He was truly selfless in prayer (John 17:11).

His prayers were always answered. "I knew that you always hear me," He affirmed (John 11:42). His assurance was based on the fact that He knew He always prayed according to the will of His Father. He refused to pray for the twelve legions of angels who would have sped to His assistance because He knew it to be contrary to God's will.

In cases where the divine will was not fully revealed, Jesus maintained an attitude of submission. "Not my will, but yours be done" (Luke 22:42). This petition shows the essence of real prayer—total surrender to the mind, will, and character of God.

From the Gospels it would appear that of all His characteristics, the prayer life of Christ impressed His disciples most deeply. They did not ask Him to teach them how to preach or heal or teach, but they did make a request that each of us could pray at this moment: "Lord, teach us to pray."

KEY INSIGHT
INTO THE LIFE AND WORK OF CHRIST

*Prayer was at the center of
the great works that Christ performed,
as well as becoming a source
of strength for weariness and sorrow.*

20

THE ANGUISH
OF CHRIST

Then he said to them, 'My soul is overwhelmed with sorrow to the point of death'" (Matthew 26:38). Eight gnarled and ancient olive trees still mark the place where this mysterious incident in the life of our Lord was enacted. It is not beyond the bounds of possibility that these very trees were silent witnesses of the anguish of the Son of God.

When F. W. Krummacher spoke of this sacred mystery of our Savior's passion, he said he felt as if at this garden gate there stood a cherub who, if not with flaming sword, yet with a repelling gesture refused admittance and emphatically repeated our Lord's command to remain outside. We stand on holy ground indeed, yet as the record is written for our instruction, we may reverently study it.

Only a few minutes before entering the garden, Jesus had offered His High Priestly Prayer (John 17). But what a striking contrast there is between those two prayers. How can the serenity of the one and the agony of the other be explained? The first prayer was intercessory; this was personal, the prelude to Calvary. Before entering the garden He had partaken of the Last Supper with His disciples, and they had joined in singing "the Hallel" (Psalms 115–118). The hearts of the disciples were heavy with foreboding. The heart of Jesus was weighed down with the anticipation of the cross.

He took with Him His three dearly loved intimate friends, that they might share with Him the midnight vigil. His sentinels slept at their post. Luke tells us that they were "sleeping for sorrow" (Luke 22:45 KJV). We should be charitable in our judgment of them, however, for their Lord did not judge them harshly. "The spirit is willing," He said, "but the body is weak" (Matthew 26:41). He commended their willingness of spirit while marveling at the weakness of the flesh in such an hour of crisis. We must remember that it was long past the retiring hour of these former fishermen, and the past few days had held tremendous emotional stress for them.

The place of His prayer was named most appropriately—Gethsemane, the oil press. Did not our Savior under the pressure of a great agony yield here precious oil that has been the balm of many a wounded soul? The garden was well known to the traitor, who had already departed on his last evil errand. Leaving His disciples, Jesus moved a little farther into the garden. "He withdrew about a stone's throw beyond them" (Luke 22:41). The word "withdrew" means literally "tore himself away," evidence of what it cost Him to leave His disciples and fight the dread battle alone. He "began to be sorrowful and troubled" (Matthew 26:37).

THE POIGNANCY OF HIS SUFFERINGS

At least six statements, each presenting a different facet of our Savior's suffering in the garden, are preserved for us in the gospel records. The strongest words in the Greek language are used to describe His anguish. Although we do not presume to understand more than a fraction of their deep emotion, they demand our reverent examination.

He became "overwhelmed with sorrow" (Matthew 26:38) and pressured. He had always been a "man of sorrows," but now He enters on sorrow so intense that everything He had suffered in the past seemed as tiny ripples when compared with the curling billows that now engulfed Him.

He "began to be . . . amazed" (Mark 14:33 KJV), utterly surprised, stunned with astonishment. "Our Lord's first feeling was one of terrified surprise," wrote H. B. Swete. "Long as He had foreseen the Passion, when it came closely into view, its terrors exceeded His anticipations. His human soul received a new experience, and the last lesson of obedience began with a sensation of inconceivable awe." As He saw the ingredients of the terrible cup that was being mixed for Him, He was dazed and overwhelmed.

He *"began to be deeply distressed and troubled"* (Mark 14:33), very troubled, with much heartache. Lightfoot suggests that the expression in this verse translated "very heavy" in the King James Version points to a confused, restless, half-distracted state. Another commentator suggests that the root idea is being "away from home," or "beside oneself." And was He not in a very real sense away from home? And did that fact not make His sufferings the more difficult?

He was *"overwhelmed with sorrow to the point of death"* (Matthew 26:38). The word used here indicates "an unfathomable depth of anguish and sorrow." The devil, who had left the Lord for a season after the encounter in the wilderness (Luke 4:13), had now returned and endeavored to terrify Him with painful things, as in the desert they were pleasurable. He had the hope of turning Him aside from His allegiance to God and truth. Since he could not allure Him, he would try to terrify Him.

The significance of the words "to the point of death" might be that the weight of sorrow and agony was so great that He feared His physical frame might collapse before He reached the cross. In order that this might not take place, God sent an angel to infuse fresh strength (Luke 22:43).

He was *"in anguish"* (Luke 22:44; "in an agony," KJV), or conflict, as the same word is rendered in Colossians 2:1 (KJV; "struggling," NIV). "And . . . he prayed more earnestly." The Hebrews epistle tells us that He prayed "with loud cries and tears" (Hebrews 5:7). As the powers of darkness closed in on Him, and the nearness of the cross pressed upon Him, He found Himself in a conflict the like of which He had never before experienced.

His sweat *"was as it were great drops of blood falling down to the ground"* (Luke 22:44 KJV). It was a cold night, but as He prayed in agony, the course of nature was reversed. The blood, instead of rushing to the aid of His overburdened and breaking heart, forced its way out through the pores to fall in great drops to the ground. We stand in awe of this evidence of His matchless love.

There will always be mystery in the agony of Gethsemane, because the mystery of the Incarnation is involved. There is no parallel between His sufferings and those of the martyrs, who were often joyful as they approached the hour of martyrdom. But there was no vicarious element in their sufferings. They suffered and died *after* He had removed the guilt and exhausted the penalty of their sins. For them there was no hiding of the Father's face.

THE INGREDIENTS OF THE CUP

These were at least three.

The renewed attack of Satan. "This is your hour, and the power of darkness," He said to the chief priests (Luke 22:53 KJV). Foiled in every previous attempt to deflect the Lord from the way of the cross, the massed powers of darkness launched a terrific blitzkrieg during the next hours in one final attempt to overthrow Him. This was no mock battle but a struggle to the death of Light with darkness.

The anticipated assumption of the guilt of a world of men. "The LORD has laid on him the iniquity of us all," spoke Isaiah prophetically of the Messiah (Isaiah 53:6). Nothing less than suffering for our sin can explain this unparalleled agony. "I believe that this view is the only reasonable solution of our Lord's agony," wrote Bishop J. C. Ryle. "The experience in the Garden is a knot which nothing can untie but the old doctrine of our sin being imputed to Christ, and Christ being made sin and a curse for us." He drank a cup of wrath without mercy, that we might drink a cup of mercy without wrath. The agony was not the fear of death but the deep sense of God's wrath against sin that He was to bear. His pure and holy nature shrank, not from death as death, but from death as a curse for the world's sin.

The anticipated averting of His Father's face. Before many hours He would be asking, "My God, my God, why have you forsaken me?"

(Matthew 27:46). It was bad enough that He should be in an alien country, about to be betrayed by His friend, deserted by His followers, denied by one of His closest disciples—and this was not hidden from His knowledge—but to be forsaken by God because He was being "made . . . to be sin for us" (2 Corinthians 5:21)! This was an utterly new and bewildering experience, the anticipation of which produced the blood-letting agony.

THE PRAYER IN GETHSEMANE

Expositors differ in their interpretation of the verse "During the days of Jesus' life on earth, he offered up prayers and petitions with loud cries and tears to the one who could save him from death, and he was heard because of his reverent submission" (Hebrews 5:7), or "for his godly fear" (RSV). In considering our Lord's petition that the cup might pass from Him, it is certain that He was not seeking some alternative to what He knew to be His Father's plan for Him. Had He not insisted on the necessity of His being uplifted on a cross? Is He now trying to escape it? Unthinkable!

Since every prayer our Lord uttered was answered (John 11:22), this prayer must have been answered, too. His reverence for His Father and His devotion to His will made it impossible that His prayers should be unanswered.

It has been suggested that a fourth ingredient in "the cup" may have been not the future cross but the possibility of death in Gethsemane before He reached Golgotha. This suggestion is based on Christ's statement as it is given in the King James Version, "My soul is exceeding sorrowful *unto death*" (Mark 14:34, italics added). If that was indeed the case, His prayer was answered by His Father's sending an angel to strengthen Him, and in the serenity with which He met the mob (Luke 22:43). His strength was renewed, and He went forward to accomplish our redemption and finally to dismiss His spirit by an act of His will. It is true that Christ is King in the realm of sorrow, peerless in His pain, supreme in His distress.

KEY INSIGHT
INTO THE LIFE AND WORK OF CHRIST

Jesus suffered great anguish in the Garden of Gethsemane because of Satan's attacks, and He assumed the guilt of all of our sins, with the knowledge that the Father would temporarily turn from Him.

21

THE TRIAL
OF CHRIST

That entire drama of tragedy," writes E. W. Westhafer, "from the arrest in the garden of Gethsemane to the last spear-thrust in His side on Golgotha, was so utterly illegal that had He but spoken one sentence of assertion of His rights, under either Jewish or Roman law, the crucifixion would never have occurred. But He did not speak, He chose His suffering."

Never were legal proceedings more irregular or a verdict more unjust than in the trial of Jesus. From arrest to crucifixion, every principle of justice was violated and provisions of both criminal and ecclesiastical law flouted.

THE ARREST

According to the laws of the Sanhedrin, the taking of any steps in criminal proceedings after sunset was expressly prohibited. The arrest that was instigated by the ecclesiastical authorities was brought about through a bribed traitor, contrary to the Mosaic Law, which prohibited the taking of a gift (Exodus 23:8). The judges themselves participated in the arrest, for some members of the Sanhedrin, in their anxiety to see that their schemes did not miscarry, had joined in the crowd that intruded on the Savior's agony in the garden.

THE ECCLESIASTICAL TRIALS

Between the arrest and the death of our Lord there were only eighteen hours, and yet much indignity and injustice were crowded into them. He stood three trials before the religious authorities—Annas, Caiaphas, and the Sanhedrin—and three trials before Pilate and Herod. Each ecclesiastical trial was illegal because it was conducted before the morning sacrifice. The trials before Annas and Caiaphas, when they sat alone, violated legal provisions (Deuteronomy 19:16–17). The requirement of two or three witnesses was conveniently ignored (Deuteronomy 17:6). Caiaphas contravened the provisions of the Mishnah by seeking to get Christ to incriminate Himself (Matthew 26:63). The Mishnah wisely provided that in a case involving capital punishment, the verdict could not be given on the same day. At least twenty-four hours must elapse between trial and verdict, thus guarding against arriving at a hasty decision.

Then, as today, secret trials were illegal. All criminal cases had to be heard in public. In this case the Sanhedrin conducted a secret trial in a private place. Jews could not hold court on a feast day any more than our courts sit on Sunday.

The charge of blasphemy against Jesus actually originated with His judges! But Dr. Edersheim points out that "the Sanhedrin did not and could not originate charges, it only investigated those that were brought before it." The witnesses against Him were known perjurers (Matthew 26:59–60), were not sworn, and their evidence was not consistent (see Deuteronomy 19:16–21).

The judges were to be humane and kind, but Caiaphas was abusive, and Jesus was struck on the mouth before any charge against Him was proved.

THE VERDICT

The function of the Jewish judge was not merely to try the case but to defend the prisoner, who was presumed to be innocent until proved guilty. Thus every accused person should be given every opportunity of establishing his innocence. There are many differences between Jewish and Western laws, and one of those is that if the vote of condemnation of the judges was unanimous, it was considered that the judges had failed in their duty of defending the accused, who would be released.

Instead of releasing Jesus, however, they unanimously condemned Him on His own unsupported testimony (Deuteronomy 19:15). The high priest defied the Levitical code by rending his garments (Leviticus 21:10). The voting in a capital case was to be individual, beginning with the younger men, lest they be influenced by the voting of their elders. In our Lord's trial, not only were His words distorted (John 2:19–21; cf. Matthew 26:60–61) and His defense not heard, but they voted simultaneously in violation of their own law (Matthew 26:66). The ecclesiastical trials were shot through with prejudice, fraud, and illegality. The religious leaders were determined to secure a conviction at all costs, whether the evidence justified it or not.

THE ROMAN TRIALS

Fearing that Jesus might appeal to Pilate, the Jews sought to forestall Him by changing their charge from blasphemy—the issue in the ecclesiastical trials, which they knew would be rejected by Pilate—to that of revolution (Luke 23:2). Jesus, they alleged, was establishing a rival empire, a charge any Roman governor must seriously examine.

The devout and legalistic Jews were too pious to enter a Gentile dwelling on a feast day! This is the ultimate instance of religious legalism going hand in hand with cruel and bloodthirsty criminality. Respecting their scruples, Pilate came out and asked, "What charges are you bringing against this man?" Their answer made clear to Pilate that they desired him not so much to dispense justice to the accused as to confirm their own condemnation of Him. Pilate said, "Take him yourselves and judge him by your own law." But this was not to their liking, for they had no power of enforcing capital punishment (John 18:31). Finally Pilate demanded a formal accusation, which they brought under three counts (Luke 23:2).

He subverted the nation.

He opposed paying taxes to Caesar.

He claimed to be their king.

The first two unsubstantiated counts were dismissed by Pilate, but the third was so serious that he could not ignore it, since it was treason against Rome.

Contrary to Roman law, however, Pilate endeavored to make the prisoner incriminate Himself. Having heard Jesus (John 18:33–37), Pilate brought the trial to an end by the pronouncement "I find no basis for a charge against him" (John 18:38).

That acquittal should have been followed by the immediate release of Jesus. Instead, it brought a fresh torrent of accusations that caused the weak Pilate to vacillate. A chance mention of Galilee afforded the welcome opportunity of passing on his problem to Herod, who had jurisdiction over that district and who by a happy chance was in Jerusalem at the moment (Luke 23:7).

Herod had long wished to see this miracle worker, but Jesus' refusal to perform to his satisfaction hurt his royal pride. Since no evidence was determined that would warrant a conviction, he contented himself with mocking Him and sent Him back to Pilate.

PILATE AND HEROD

A significant sentence occurs in Luke's record of that momentous day. "That day Herod and Pilate became friends" (Luke 23:12). Why? Secular history supplies the answer. Pilate and Herod, it appears, were fellow conspirators against Caesar, hence Pilate's concern when the Jews said, "If you let this man go, you are no friend of Caesar" (John 19:12). Had news of his participation in the conspiracy leaked out? He must not do anything that would seem in any way disloyal to Caesar. The prisoner (whether innocent or guilty matters not) must be sacrificed to save his own skin.

Then followed a violation of the law as well as a violation of justice. Pilate resorted to every strategy to secure the release of Jesus and yet not imperil his own position at Rome. He endeavored to get the Jews to consent to His release, since none of the charges against Him had been substantiated, but all to no avail. They would be appeased by nothing less than blood. Barabbas the murderer was much to be preferred to Jesus the sinless Son of God. Though declared innocent, He was scourged, clothed in purple, and crowned with thorns. Only at the end did the true charge come to the surface. "We have a law," cried the Jews, "and according to that law he must die, because *he claimed to be the Son of God*" (John 19:7, italics added).

At last the cowardly Pilate succumbed to their threats and delivered Him up to be crucified. But as Maclaren points out, he took his revenge by placing upon the cross the announcement that was so galling to them, "The king of the Jews." Then he washed his hands, according to the Jewish custom, saying, "I am innocent of the blood of this righteous man" (Matthew 27:24 ASV). "His blood be on us and on our children" was their fateful response.

On what legal grounds was Jesus condemned? None! He was tried six times and acquitted three times, and yet was condemned to die. The Light of the World had shone with such a searching beam that a guilty world must try to extinguish it.

THE IMPORTANCE OF THE TRIAL

Wherein does its importance consist? "It lies in the fact," says W. Robertson Nicoll, "that the issue raised was Christ's claim to be the Son of God, the Messiah of Israel, and a King. He was tried unfairly and judged unjustly, but the true issue was raised. He died, then, because before the Jews He claimed to be the Son of God and the Messiah, and before Pilate to be Christ and King."

All generations since have felt that the judged was the Judge. The men were really standing before the judgment seat of Christ, and all appear with their many failings as revealed by the Light of the World.

143

KEY INSIGHT
INTO THE LIFE AND WORK OF CHRIST

*The One who was judged
and given the harshest punishment
for calling Himself the
Son of God will one day
be the judge of all men.*

22

THE MAJESTIC
SILENCE OF CHRIST

With the background of our Lord's trial and all its irregularities and illegalities, His silence is all the more vocal. His bearing and His responses during those proceedings were worthy of His Father. He maintained the dignified calm and the loving forbearance that had always characterized Him.

An examination of the gospel records reveals His demeanor.

HIS DIGNIFIED BEARING

Throughout the trumped-up and biased proceedings of His trial, Jesus was never other than calm and dignified. No matter how great the provocation, He never descended to abuse or retaliation. Even when struck in the face by a servant of the high priest simply because He had rightly suggested the need of calling witnesses to establish the Sanhedrin's case, Jesus replied with dignity and restraint. He merely asked the servant and, by extension, the entire ecclesiastical court, "If I spoke the truth, why did you strike me?" (John 18:23).

The priests were endeavoring to make Him appear a secret instigator of rebellion, and His only response was to call attention to the fact that He always acted openly, as a hundred witnesses could testify (vv. 20–21).

A comparison of Paul's reaction under almost identical circumstances is very revealing. Paul could not resist hurling back a stinging rejoinder that conveyed his contempt and indignation (Acts 23:3). He lost his temper, but Jesus maintained a sublime calm.

HIS ELOQUENT SILENCE

It is always more difficult to remain silent than to speak. But on three occasions it is recorded of the Lord that He was silent before His enemies: first, before the Jewish rulers (Matthew 26:62–63; Mark 14:61), second, before Pilate (Mark 15:3–5), and third, before Herod (Luke 23:8–11). In each case His silence was immeasurably more eloquent than any spoken word could possibly have been.

When *the bitterly prejudiced Sanhedrin* with its perjured witnesses endeavored to make Him incriminate Himself, *"Jesus remained silent"* (Matthew 26:63, italics added). He listened in silence to the witnesses contradicting each other but volunteered no reply to the high priest's interruption.

"Are you not going to answer? What is this testimony that these men are bringing against you?" he thundered. Before those clear, searching eyes the high priest became ill at ease. But asserting his right, he said to Jesus, "I charge you under oath by the living God: Tell us if you are the Christ, the Son of God" (Matthew 26:62–63). Now they were at the heart of the matter, and in those words was clearly revealed the true purpose of the trial. If he could get Jesus to assert His deity, then He was in their power.

Only then did the Lord choose to open His mouth, for His continued silence could then be construed as a decision to withdraw His claims. Knowing that His answer would without doubt seal His doom, Jesus answered, "Yes, it is as you say." But He added these prophetic words, "In the future you will see the Son of Man sitting at the right hand of the Mighty One and coming on the clouds of heaven" (Matthew 26:64). It was as if to say, "You are My judges now, but the hour is coming when roles will be reversed, and it will be you who will stand before My bar to answer for your action in condemning Me."

When He appeared *before Pontius Pilate* with the chief priests vehemently bringing charges against Him, He answered nothing. "'Aren't you going to answer?'" questioned Pilate. "'See how many things they are accusing you of.' But Jesus still made no reply, and Pilate was amazed" (Mark 15:3–5). Conscious of His complete integrity, Jesus ignored both judge and accusers, to the discomfort of both. His silence was more crushing than any words He could speak.

"In the silence of this interior hall," wrote James Stalker, "He and Pilate stood face to face, He in the lonely prisoner's place, Pilate in the place of power. Yet how strangely, as we look back at the scene, are the places reversed. It is Pilate who is going to be tried. All that morning Pilate is being judged and exposed; and ever since he has stood in the pillory of history, with the centuries gazing at him."

Before Herod, whom Jesus called "that fox" (Luke 13:32), Jesus maintained a similar lofty silence. The corrupt king welcomed the diversion created by the appearance of Jesus. He had long desired to see this man of whom he had heard so much perform some miracle. Herod "plied him with many questions, but Jesus *gave him no answer*" (Luke 23:9, italics added). Herod's many words met only a calm and impressive silence that was very disconcerting for the king and the chief priests and scribes who strongly accused Him.

Jesus had counseled His disciples not to waste their pearls of truth on those who would not appreciate them (Matthew 7:6), and He was practicing His own precept. Herod was merely seeking entertainment, and Jesus refused to gratify his vulgar desire. Such silence in the face of certain death was the hallmark of His inner courage and strength.

HIS CONSISTENT CLAIMS

Throughout the crowded closing hours of His life, Jesus did and said nothing that could in any way be construed as a withdrawal or watering-down of the astounding claims to kingship and deity He had made. Although He did not disallow the claim that He was King, He hastened to make clear that His kingdom was not of this world but was a spiritual one (John 18:36). Nor did He deny that He was "the Christ, the Son of the Blessed One" (Mark 14:61) but quietly accepted the title. In the face of such a statement, it is difficult to understand how hostile critics can suggest as they do that He never claimed deity for Himself. He always spoke and acted in a manner entirely consistent with such a claim.

HIS SUBLIME INDIFFERENCE

Nothing could be more impressive than His total indifference to the insults and threats of His unscrupulous judges. For various reasons Pilate obviously desired to release Jesus, but He did nothing to make it easy for Pilate to do so, or to assist him in this goal. He was an unusual prisoner.

When Pilate suggested that he would listen favorably to Him, much to the governor's amazement, Jesus did not even try to answer. He showed not the slightest interest in Pilate's repeated endeavors to secure His release, whether by dissuading the Jews from pressing their demand or by persuading them to accept Barabbas the murderer instead of Jesus the Holy One.

When for the last time Pilate sought to release Jesus, he said, "Do you refuse to speak to me? . . . Don't you realize I have power either to free you or to crucify you?" (John 19:10). Jesus answered, "You would have no power over me if it were not given to you from above." Both by His silence and His words, Jesus made clear that it was Pilate and the Jews who were on trial before Him, and not He before them.

HIS PERFECT COMPOSURE

The moving words of Robert E. Speer complete the picture:

He said but little, but He said enough, and no word of His ever bore testimony to the truth, or revealed more fully the majesty of His divine life than the uncomplaining patience and self-possession and composure of His conduct under the hideous treatment to which He was subjected; when after His condemnation before Caiaphas, the men who held Him, in pretence that He was a dangerous character spit in His face and mocked Him, and beat Him, and blindfolding Him, struck and reviled Him. "Prophesy unto us, Thou Christ: who is he that struck thee?" When Herod with his soldiers set Him at nought and made sport of Him and sent Him back through the streets of the city arrayed in mock royal attire, and became the friend of Pilate again through this sport—cursed be such friendships. When in the hope, doubtless, of showing the people how harmless and inoffensive He was, Pilate had Him brought before the people with the jeering remark, "Behold the Man!" When, after the surrender of Pilate, the whole band of the governor's soldiers took Him, stripped, put on Him a scarlet robe, with a crown of acanthus thorns still piercing His brow and staining His face crimson like His robe, and giving Him a reed for a scep-tre, played with Him as a mock king, spitting on Him and seizing His sceptre from His hand and smiting Him on the head with it, driving the thorn's cruel spikes deeper into His brow; when at last they led Him away to Calvary, stripped of His robe, but still wearing His crown.

"Behold the man!" was Pilate's jeer. That is what all the ages have been doing since, and the vision has grown more and more glorious. As they have looked, the crown of thorns has become a crown of golden ra-diance, and the cast-off robe has glistened like the garments He wore on the night of the Transfiguration. Martyrs have smiled in the flames at that vision, sinners have turned at it to a new life . . . and towards it the souls of men yearn forever.

KEY INSIGHT
INTO THE LIFE AND WORK OF CHRIST

Jesus was not to be shaken by the insults, threats, and deceptions of the Jewish rulers and sometimes chose to remain silent so as not to dignify their attacks.

23

THE ATONING
WORK OF CHRIST

I n the words "The Son of God . . . loved me, and gave himself for me"
(Galatians 2:20 KJV) lies the heart of the Atonement. In love, the Son
of God literally gave *Himself for me*. This puts in personal terms the great
transaction of Calvary. It is as true today as when it happened. In-
exhaustible in depth and meaning it may be, but it is neither irrational
nor beyond comprehension when the illumination of the Spirit is present.

In the three simple words *Himself for me* is enshrined the great mystery of the ages. The forfeiting of His free life has freed our forfeited lives.
The most astute intellects of all time have delved into the inner meaning of Christ's death on the cross, but all have failed to plumb its infinite depths. Like Paul, they have withdrawn with the cry of bafflement.
"O the depth of the riches both of the wisdom and knowledge of God!
how unsearchable are his judgments, and his ways past finding out!" (Romans 11:33 KJV). The sin of the first Adam posed a stupendous problem. How could God justify guilty men and women without condoning
their sin and violating His own holiness? It was a problem to which
only His own infinite wisdom could find a solution.

"At the cross, God took the initiative," wrote James Denney, "and
so dealt with sin in His Son, that now He can justify the repenting sinner and not compromise His holy character."

The death of our Lord was unlike every other death. It was not an incident in His life but the very purpose of it. His self-sacrifice was no accident in a brilliant career; it was the chosen vocation of the God-man.

It is obviously impossible to condense into a few paragraphs the teaching of Scripture concerning this most profound of all mysteries, so in this chapter we shall merely try to present what seem to be some of the main features of the Atonement.

THEORIES OF THE ATONEMENT

Theories of the Atonement abound, but most are the product of man's speculation rather than the careful exegesis of all the relevant Scriptures. Many of them appear to have been formulated in an attempt, not so much to ascertain the teaching of Scripture on the subject as to evade the real issue involved in the doctrine—the fact that there is something in the nature of God that required payment for sin, and that the death of Jesus was the death of a substitute. Few of these theories are without some errors. They often arise in a laudable attempt to remove from this doctrine the strict, legal, and almost mechanical manner in which it has sometimes been presented.

It is my firm belief that any attempt to reduce Christ's sufferings in Gethsemane and at Calvary to anything less than a substitution on our behalf is to interpret them superficially and ignore large tracts of Scripture teaching. Many theories emphasize a partial truth, but they cannot stand alone because they fail to present an adequate explanation of that great event or to satisfactorily explain the key Scriptures relating to it. It is true that there are many differing aspects of the Atonement: for example, as a moral influence, as expressing God's moral government, as victory over sin and the devil. But despite the elements of truth in some of these theories, even taken together they are not a satisfying explanation of that great transaction if the element of substitution is excluded.

One writer expressed it as his belief that every theory concerning the death of Christ that can be understood only by the highly educated must be false. Christ's testimony concerning His own ministry was to have the Gospel preached unto the poor (Luke 4:18). All modern gospels that omit the great central truth of substitution prevent the message from being of any use to the great mass of mankind, for there are multitudes who cannot comprehend anything that is highly metaphysical.

According to W. H. Griffith Thomas, in order to be satisfactory, any theory of the Atonement must include and account for these three factors:

1. The adequate exegesis of New Testament teaching, both toward God and toward man. Every theory must start with the Godward side or it will go wrong (Romans 3:25).
2. The proper and adequate interpretation of the Old Testament sacrificial system.
3. The full meaning of Christian experience. One of the great essentials is a working theory adequate to the experience of ordinary men and women.

METHODS OF PRESENTATION

In presenting a truth of such vast reach and with such tremendous implications, the Holy Spirit employs a variety of figures of speech, each of which emphasizes a fresh facet of truth. Here are some.

The Atonement is moral in character, for it originates in and displays the glorious love of God, which is unselfish and totally free of self-seeking motives. This love, as manifested in the voluntary death of His only Son, is a source of moral stimulus to man and has broken the resistance of the hardest hearts (Hebrews 2:9; 1 John 4:9).

It is represented as a commercial transaction. It is a ransom paid to free men from the slavery of sin. In those passages which represent Christ's death as the price paid for our deliverance from sin and death, the language of bargain and exchange is used (Matthew 20:28; 1 Timothy 2:6).

It has a legal significance, for Christ's death was an act of obedience to the law that sinning men had violated (Galatians 4:4–5; Matthew 3:15). It was a penalty borne in order to rescue the guilty from their merited punishment (Romans 4:25).

It is healing in its effects. In Scripture sin is frequently represented as a hereditary and contagious disease (Isaiah 1:5–6), for which Christ's atoning death provided a cure (Isaiah 53:5; 1 Peter 2:24). Jesus Himself presented His work under this figure (Matthew 9:12–13).

It is sacrificial in nature. The Atonement is described as a work of priestly mediation that reconciles man to God (Hebrews 9:11–12, 14, 22, 26). This is the consistent and prevailing conception throughout both Old and New Testaments. Hence any view of the Atonement that does not provide a sufficient place for this aspect is inadequate.

It is popular in some theological circles to claim to have no theory of the Atonement. It is unnecessary, it is said, since it is the *fact* of the Atonement that saves, and not any theory about the fact. That sounds plausible, but it is frankly impossible. As Gresham Machen once said, one cannot believe with an empty head. One must have some comprehension of what was accomplished on the cross. The epistle to the Romans sets forth not only the fact but also the inner meaning of the Atonement.

SUBSTITUTIONARY, OR VICARIOUS, ATONEMENT

This view of the Atonement may be summarized in the words of F. F. Bruce: "At the cross, all the sin of the ages was placed on the heart of the sinless Son of God, as He became the racial representative of all humanity." This is the only theory that meets all the conditions suggested above, and it is the true Bible doctrine.

Although not a Bible word, *substitution* is certainly a Bible idea. By substitution we do not mean the saving of a life by *mere assistance,* as in the throwing of a rope to a drowning man; or by the *mere risking* of one life to save another; it is the saving of one life by the *loss* of another. As substitute, Christ took on Himself the sinner's guilt and bore its penalty in the sinner's place.

Substitution is a law of nature as well as of grace. Before there can be harvest, the grain of wheat must fall into the ground and die (John 12:24). The lion lives only because a weaker animal has died. This law can be seen in operation the world over.

It is the teaching of Scripture that there are two principles in God. They are the principles of love and justice. The former desires to save sinners. But since God is the eternal, infinite, and ethically perfect being, He cannot and will not violate His justice. Some way must be found for mercy and justice to meet—and this they did in the transaction of the Cross.

When approached without preconceived theories, the Scriptures relating to this subject appear clear and unequivocal. Christ taught His disciples that He came to give His life "a ransom for many" (Matthew 20:28). He told them He would give His flesh and blood for the life of the world (John 6:51–55). He said that as the Good Shepherd He would give His life for the sheep (John 10:11), and the Great Shepherd of the sheep did actually take the place of the sheep. He said that His blood would be shed for the many (Matthew 26:28). This is also the consistent teaching of the Epistles.

Of many examples, these three are presented:

He who knew no sin was made sin *for us* (2 Corinthians 5:21).

He who was under no curse was made a curse *for us* (Galatians 3:13).

He who had done no sin, bore *our* sin in His own body on the tree (1 Peter 2:22, 24).

OBJECTIONS TO THE SUBSTITUTIONARY IDEA

Among the objections advanced to the foregoing view of the Atonement are these:

It is unnecessary, since God might well forgive sinners upon repentance and without any additional requirements.

But is the objector really assuming for himself the knowledge of God? Who can say what God can or cannot do? And is repentance in fact all that is necessary to forgiveness? Does it remove the consequences of sin? In ordinary life, does repentance ward off just punishment or remove past guilt? Though repentance is necessary to forgiveness, it is not all that is necessary. Do not the sacrifices offered by men the world over bear testimony to the universal awareness that sin demands the punishment of the offender or the death of a substitute? And in the act of forgiveness, is it not the one against whom the offense has been committed who suffers?

It is impossible, for guilt cannot be transferred from one person to another, nor can punishment and penalty be transferred from a guilty person to an innocent person. An innocent person may suffer, but his suffering will not be punishment or penalty.

It may be true that punishment for personal wrong cannot be transferred from the wrongdoer to the well doer. But the world is constructed in a way that it bears the idea of substitution engraved on its very heart. Wives suffer to deliver husbands from sufferings richly deserved. Are we wrong in teaching what Christ Himself taught, that He suffered in order to deliver us from sufferings we richly deserved?

Another objection is that *it is immoral* for the innocent to suffer for the guilty.

Our answer is that if this is the case, then sympathy is immoral, and love too. It is not immoral for the innocent to suffer for the guilty when the innocent One by His own free will assumes the burden (Hebrews 10:7) and retains the power to relinquish it at will (John 10:18). Since Christ did this voluntarily, no injustice is done to anyone. Nor is it immoral when He has power to bear the penalty to the maximum and, having exhausted it, to be free Himself and bring deliverance to others. This redemption scheme provided an ample and unparalleled reward. "Looking unto Jesus the author and finisher of our faith; who for the joy that was set before him endured the cross, despising the shame, and is set down at the right hand of the throne of God" (Hebrews 12:2 KJV; cf. Philippians 2:8–11).

Is it possible that an immoral doctrine should be the supreme cause of morality among men? History witnesses that the great moral advances of the human race have been brought about by the preaching of substitutionary atonement.

It is a matter of question whether those who deny the element of substitution in the death of Christ reflect deeply on the logical consequences of their denial. There are only two possible alternatives presented in Scripture. Either Christ bore the burden and penalty of our sin, or we bear it. There is no middle way. To deny that Christ bore our sins in His body on the cross means that the idea of Christianity as a *redemptive* religion must be abandoned.

The vicarious view of the Atonement is not an optional alternative, one of several interesting theories that can be adopted or rejected at will. The evidence of Scripture is that this view lies at the very heart of the Atonement.

The words of J. S. Stewart find the fullest support in Scripture. "Not only had Christ by dying disclosed the sinner's guilt, not only had He revealed the Father's love: He had actually taken the sinner's place. And this meant, since 'God was in Christ,' that God had taken that place. When destruction and death were rushing up to claim the sinner as their prey, Christ had stepped in and accepted the full weight of their inevitable doom in His body and soul."

KEY INSIGHT
INTO THE LIFE AND WORK OF CHRIST

To understand the atoning work of Christ, we must understand what God did, in light of the Old Testament sacrificial system, and how this experience enters into the totality of our lives.

24

WORDS OF
COMFORT

L ast words are always impressive, especially when they come from
the lips of one dearly loved. The atmosphere of the approaching
end charges them with added solemnity and meaning. In the light of eternity, the trivial and nonessential are usually abandoned. It is recorded that
when Lord William Russell mounted the scaffold, he took his watch from
his pocket and gave it to Dr. Burnett with the remark, "I have no further use for this. My thoughts are in eternity."

Because they were Christ's last words, and spoken under such tragic
circumstances, the seven sayings of our Lord from the pulpit of the cross
are of special significance. In them He laid bare His inmost soul, and in
them He exemplified the spiritual principles He had been teaching. They
are a luminous interpretation of His sufferings and for this reason are
included in our study.

It is significant that He spoke seven times from the cross—a complete interpretation of the stupendous event that was being enacted. Each
of these sayings is an ocean of truth compressed into a drop of speech and
warrants close and reverent study. It is to be expected that utterances on
a cross would be staccato, and yet that monstrous moment was transformed into the most eloquent pulpit of the ages.

In this chapter we shall consider the first through the third of the last words of Christ; in the next chapter we shall consider the fourth through the seventh words.

PART I: THE WORD OF FORGIVENESS

"When they came to the place called the Skull, there they crucified him, along with the criminals—one on his right, the other on his left. Jesus said, 'Father, forgive them, for they do not know what they are doing'" (Luke 23:33–34).

"Forgive them." To whom did our Lord intend His prayer to apply? There are varying views. One scholar applies it to the Romans, another to the Jews, another to both Jews and Gentiles, and still another scholar to all mankind. Is it too much to think that His petition included not only those around the cross but also the world of sinful men? Are we not all implicated in the death of Christ? Was it not the sin of the world that nailed Him to the cross? At the very moment of His prayer He was dying that the sins of all men might be cleansed.

"For they do not know what they are doing." It seems as though He was trying to find some extenuating circumstance that might lessen their guilt. His sense of justice was not held back by His agony, and He assigned degrees of guilt. This plea limits His "forgive them," so that Judas and Pilate and some of the religious leaders are excluded from the benefits of His intercession. Unlike the majority, they had not acted in ignorance. Judas and Pilate knew what they were doing. They had both weighed Jesus' claims and had acted deliberately. But to the minds of many of the Jews, blinded by hatred, Jesus was no more than a blasphemous impostor. He therefore cried out that their action was due to ignorance not of the *fact* of their crime but of *its enormity.*

In keeping with our Lord's plea, Peter later said to his own kinsmen, "I know that you acted in ignorance, as did your leaders" (Acts 3:17). Paul too conceded that if "they had [understood it], they would not have crucified the Lord of glory" (1 Corinthians 2:8). But their ignorance did not excuse their guilt, or Christ would not have needed to pray, "Forgive them." Even those who did not know needed forgiveness. Ignorance may mitigate the criminality of sin, but it never exonerates. Their ignorance did not make their sin excusable, but it meant that they themselves were forgivable.

"We must beware of supposing," wrote Bishop J. C. Ryle, "that ignorance is not blameworthy, and that ignorant persons *deserve* to be forgiven for their sins. At this rate ignorance would be a desirable thing. All spiritual ignorance is more or less culpable. It is part of man's sin that he does not know better than he does. On the other hand we cannot fail to observe in Scripture that sins of ignorance are less sinful before God than sins of knowledge, and that no case is so apparently hopeless as that of the man who sins willfully against the light."

The sacrificial system of the Old Testament and the New Testament commentary on it make clear that in God's sight atonement is just as necessary for sins of ignorance as for sins of willfulness. God never scales down His demands to the level of our ignorance. In grace He does have compassion on the ignorant, as Paul himself testified: "I was shown mercy because I acted in ignorance and unbelief" (1 Timothy 1:13).

The example. It is instructive to note the uniqueness of our Lord here as everywhere else. Stephen, the first Christian martyr, noble though he was, falls far below the standard of his martyr-Lord. Stephen thought first of himself and only then of his enemies. "While they were stoning him, Stephen prayed, 'Lord Jesus, receive my spirit.' Then he fell on his knees and cried out, 'Lord, do not hold this sin against them'" (Acts 7:59–60).

PART II: THE WORD OF ASSURANCE

"I tell you the truth, today you will be with me in paradise" (Luke 23:43).

Three men were hanging upon three crosses. All three appeared to be criminals, for around the neck of each hung a board on which was written a record of their crimes. Two of them were patriots, doubtless associates of Barabbas in his ill-starred insurrection. In order to achieve their ends, they had resorted to robbery and even to murder.

And the One on the center cross, what was His crime? Surely something revolting for Him to be found in such company. Yet the record of His life is strangely out of keeping with such a character: "He went around doing good" (Acts 10:38). "All . . . were amazed at the gracious words that came from his lips" (Luke 4:22).

One of the most incredible facts of the whole event is that those seasoned criminals became anxious for their reputations through being crucified in His company! Lest they be credited with being His friends or associates, they joined company with the passersby, the chief priests, scribes, and elders. As they taunted and mocked Him, the thieves "cast the same in his teeth" (Matthew 27:44 KJV). Hurling their abuse at a fellow sufferer when they were so near their own end indicated the depths of their depravity. Their animosity toward One who had done them no ill was a revealing demonstration of the enmity toward God of the carnal mind (Romans 8:7).

Then a sudden change came over one of the thieves. Had he been a spectator of what transpired in Jesus' trial before Pilate? Had he been so impressed by the contrast between his companion and Christ that he could explain it only on the basis of deity? Had the Holy Spirit in response to his penitence revealed our Lord's true identity to him?

The Scripture does not say, but the suppositions may be true. In any case, he turned on his brother robber: "Don't you fear God, . . . since you are under the same sentence? We are punished justly, for we are getting what our deeds deserve. But this man has done nothing wrong." Then, turning to Jesus, he pleaded, "Jesus, remember me when you come into your kingdom" (Luke 23:40–42).

If the first word from the cross was the intercession of our Lord as High Priest, praying for the forgiveness of those who crucified Him, this second, in response to the thief at His side, was His promise as King of Glory: "I tell you the truth, today you will be with me in paradise."

It should be noted that Jesus did not answer the exact petition of the thief. He did something better. He granted the desire of his heart. The thief little knew that his request, as he had worded it, postponed the desired boon for the two millennia or more that would elapse before Christ came into His kingdom.

Among others, these comforting truths emerge from this word from the cross.

The survival of the soul after the death of the body. One writer has pointed out that each of the seven sayings from the cross is the deathblow of an error. This word refutes the dogma of soul-sleep. Death is no sleep of the soul. Death is not the end of life but the gateway to new life. It also deals a deathblow to the doctrine of purgatory. If ever a man needed the cleansing of the purgatorial flame, it was this man.

The separate existence of soul and body. "With me." The body of the thief was not in the tomb with that of Christ, but his soul was in conscious presence with Him in the place of departed spirits. This was Paul's long-ing. "I desire to depart and be *with Christ,* which is better by far" (Philippians 1:23, italics added). What a joyous anticipation—not unconscious sleep but conscious union. If the dead are unconscious, this assurance would afford little comfort.

The sudden entry of the redeemed upon the bliss of eternity. "Today." Anderson Berry points out a correspondence between the thief's request and Christ's response. The *form* of the response appears to be designed to match in its *order* of thought the robber's petition.

And he said to Jesus
And Jesus said to him

Lord
Verily I say unto thee

Remember me
Shalt thou be with me

When thou comest
Today

Into Thy Kingdom
In Paradise
—Author Unknown

By this arrangement of the words, it is seen that "today" is the emphatic word. "Absent from the body, present with the Lord." Not purgatory but paradise.

The Savior's prompt response to penitence. Our Lord can never resist the plea of a penitent sinner. To the taunts and jeers of the mob He gave no answer, but the plea of the repentant thief drew an immediate response.

The thief asked only a place in Christ's memory. He was granted a place in His kingdom.

PART III: THE WORD OF DEVOTION

"When Jesus saw his mother there, and the disciple whom he loved standing nearby, he said to his mother, 'Dear woman, here is your son,' and to the disciple, 'Here is your mother.' From that time on, this disciple took her into his home" (John 19:26–27).

Mother-love illustrated. "Near the cross of Jesus stood his mother" (John 19:25). Where else would one expect to find such a mother? It was her very own Son who was suffering. The outstretched arms and nail-torn hands once had clung around her neck. The head now tortured with a crown of thorns was once pillowed on her breast. The mouth on which she had once lavished her kisses of love was now parched and swollen. Though powerless to help, she could at least be beside Him in loyalty and love.

Sympathetically she entered into all His sufferings. The spear would pierce her heart as it rent His flesh. With joy she had followed His career, had feared and prayed for Him, had rejoiced in His successes and wept over His disappointments. But now He was dying as a criminal, not as a hero! What an end to the life of such a Son! Lest she add to His sufferings, she did not give way to uncontrolled weeping but repressed her grief as the sword pierced her soul. She did not faint or swoon; she "stood." He had enough suffering of His own without her adding to His overflowing cup of sorrow.

Filial devotion exemplified. "When Jesus saw his mother there, . . . he said to his mother, 'Dear woman, here is your son.'" Our Lord's use of the word "woman" implied no disrespect. It is rather the equivalent of our "lady." One suggestion concerning its use is that Jesus did not call her "mother," lest identification with Him should expose her to insult, a suggestion in keeping with His innate courtesy and considerateness.

There is a yet deeper significance in Jesus' refusal to use the word "mother," the word above all others she would be longing to hear once again from His lips. Jesus was breaking to her the painful truth that henceforth the special relationship between them no longer obtained. From that moment she could be to Him no more than any other woman. He must have no rival in His mediatorial ministry. Was this the sharpest shaft that pierced her heart? But after Pentecost she was to have sweet compensation when she discovered that she had been led from the natural union *with Jesus* to the mystical union *with Christ*.

In every relationship of life Jesus was the pattern Man. As child and as man He always honored His father and mother. His last thought was to make suitable provision for the one from whom He had derived His human nature. Her husband was dead. He could no longer make provision for her Himself. His brothers were evidently still unbelieving. He had nothing to give her. Mary would find a congenial home with the disciple who dearly loved Him. These two, of similar temperament and united by a common love, would be able to live over again together the hallowed days of His companionship and derive comfort from their recollection.

This word from the cross marks the close of the human aspect of His work. He had prayed for His enemies; He had given assurance and comfort to the penitent thief; He had made loving provision for the care of His mother. Soon the veil of darkness would fall as He entered upon the last, the most costly phase of His atoning work.

KEY INSIGHT
INTO THE LIFE AND WORK OF CHRIST

In His words of comfort, Jesus forgives those who have hated Him, offers assurance of paradise to the thief on the cross beside Him, and remembers the needs of His mother.

25

WORDS OF CONSUMMATION

The first three words from the cross were addressed to men. Now Jesus addresses Himself to God. For the previous three hours His Father had shrouded the sun in kindly darkness. His body had been exposed to the burning rays of the pitiless Eastern sun. During the three hours of darkness His soul had been exposed to the merciless assaults of the powers of evil. Worse, infinitely worse than that, He had for the first time experienced the averted face of His Father. At the end of the sixth hour, the moment when He reached the very nadir of His misery, He broke the silence with a shuddering cry of desolation.

PART IV: THE WORD OF DERELICTION

"Jesus cried out in a loud voice, 'Eloi, Eloi, lama sabachthani?'—which means, 'My God, my God, why have you forsaken me?'" (Matthew 27:46).

"My God, my God." G. Campbell Morgan wrote: "There is no experience of life through which men pass so terrible as that of silence and mystery, the hours of isolation and sorrow when there is no voice, no vision, no sympathy, no promise, no hope, no explanation; the hours in which the soul asks, why? There is no agony for the human soul like that of silence. . . . When I am asked for a theory of the atonement, I

reply that in the midst of the mighty movement the Lord Himself said, 'why?' and if He asked that question, I dare not imagine that I can ever explain the deep central verities of His mystery of pain."

It was no new experience for the Lord to find Himself forsaken. His own brothers neither believed in Him nor followed Him. His fellow citizens in Nazareth had tried to kill Him. The nation to which He came would not receive Him. Many of His disciples went back and no longer walked with Him. Judas betrayed Him. Peter denied Him. "Then *everyone* deserted him and fled" (Mark 14:50).

But in this cry it is as though He was saying, "I can understand my kinsmen and fellow citizens and my nation forsaking Me, for darkness has no fellowship with light. I can even understand My own disciples, because of the weakness of the flesh, forsaking Me. But this is My agonizing problem, 'Why did *You* forsake Me?'"

Up till this moment, when He was forsaken by men He had been able to turn to His Father, *but now* even that refuge is denied Him, and He is absolutely *alone*. Who can plumb the depths of that anguish?

"Forsaken me." When an expression is sought to describe a scene of utmost desolation, it is termed "God-forsaken." The word means the forsaking of someone in a state of defeat or helplessness, in the midst of hostile circumstances. Who can assess the content of that word when applied to our Lord? A child forsaken by its parents, a friend forsaken by a friend in the hour of need—those are poignant enough sorrows. But a man forsaken by his God! And what shall we say of the sinless Son of Man when He was forsaken by the God with whom He had enjoyed eternal fellowship?

For the first time, an eternity of communion had been broken. The wrath of hell had already broken upon His soul in wave upon wave, but now it is the wrath of heaven! The psalmist claimed, "I have never seen the righteous forsaken" (Psalm 37:25), but the only One who was truly righteous is now forsaken. Ineffable love made Him willing to endure even this desolation of soul for our salvation.

Personal grief brought this personal cry from Him. There would be no mystery in God's forsaking us, for we would be receiving only "the due reward of our deeds" (Luke 23:41 KJV). But why should God forsake His Son who "knew no sin," "did no sin," "in whom was no sin," the Son in whom He testified that He found perfect delight? There is only one explanation. He was taking my place—and yours. He was being forsaken that we might be forgiven.

PART V: THE WORD OF AGONY

"Jesus knowing that all things were now accomplished, that the scripture might be fulfilled, saith, I thirst" (John 19:28 KJV).

An example of fulfilled prophecy. Now, even in the hour of extreme agony, His mind was free to travel the well-trodden paths of sacred Scripture. He had prayed for the pardon of His enemies. He had made provision for His mother's future. And now, as He reviewed the crowded events of the past few hours and the thirty years that had preceded them, He had the assurance that the task He had come to do was accomplished. Every prediction of Scripture concerning the Messiah had been fulfilled in Him—except one.

Up until now He had accepted His sufferings with noble silence. But in the prophetic word of the psalmist, He saw an indication of His Father's will. Had not the psalmist written, "They put gall in my food and gave me vinegar for my thirst" (Psalm 69:21)? Then it would not be contrary to His Father's will if He gave vocal expression to His physical agony. Perhaps, even among the callous soldiers at the foot of His cross, there might be one who would alleviate this burning thirst.

When hungry in the wilderness, He had resisted the seduction of the devil and had refused to perform a miracle for His own benefit, for He had no indication of His Father's will. But now He was free to open His parched lips and cry, "I thirst!" Thus the prophecy was fulfilled.

An exhibition of self-control. Only once did a cry of pain come from Him during the long, excruciating ordeal, and then it required the recognition of His Father's expressed will to open His mouth. No plea for sympathy or word of complaint crossed His lips. He lost Himself in care for others and in communion with His Father.

Suffering does not always sanctify us. It sours some people's tempers

169

and makes them selfish and demanding. This is the sin of some invalids —to become absorbed in their own miseries and to make all about them the slaves of their whims. But many triumph nobly over their temptations and follow the example of the suffering Savior.

Did Christ not thirst to be thirsted after? He still thirsts for the fellowship and devotion of those for whom He thirsted on the cross. His was a thirst that could satisfy the thirst of the whole world.

"I was thirsty and you gave me something to drink," He said to His surprised listeners. "Lord, when did we see you . . . thirsty and give you something to drink?" they replied in amazement. "Whatever you did for one of the least of these brothers of mine, you did for me" (Matthew 25:35, 37, 40).

PART VI: THE WORD OF TRIUMPH

"When Jesus therefore had received the vinegar, he said, It is finished" (John 19:30 KJV).

Suffering was ended. Some have read Christ's "It is finished" as a cry of despair, "It is all up! I have tried and failed!" But that is exactly the reverse of its meaning. True, there was a sigh of relief in that the anxiety of the cross was now over and that His absence from His heavenly home was now at an end. He knew that never again would He experience the turning away of His Father and that the burden of a world's sin had been removed. There was no note of disappointment or despair in this cry.

To Him it had been a foregone conclusion that He must suffer and that He would bear the accumulated guilt and sin of a lost world. He would experience the loneliness and rejection, the sneering and scoffing, the physical agony and mental anguish which were part of His taking on our humanity and our guilt. The cup of suffering was indeed full for Him, and as Maclaren aptly puts it, "Having drained the cup, He held it up inverted when He said 'It is finished!' and not a drop trickled down the edge. He drank it all that we might never need to drink it."

The Father's will was fulfilled. Of all mankind, Jesus alone at the close of life could say, "It is finished!" Early in His ministry He had claimed, "My food . . . is to do the will of him who sent me *and to finish his work*"

(John 4:34, italics added). At the close of His ministry He claimed, "*I have finished the work* which thou gavest me to do" (John 17:4 KJV, italics added). He alone could review His whole life with approval, aware that in every detail His Father's will had been faithfully carried out. He had done what the first Adam had failed to do—He had kept the law of God perfectly and so obtained a righteousness that is now available for all who believe in Him.

Compare our Lord's triumphant words with the great Cecil Rhodes's cry of frustration as he lay dying: "So much to do, so little done." Christ entertained no regrets, for no ground for regret existed.

Satan was defeated. The continued conflict between God and Satan forms the unifying theme of the Scriptures. From the very hour of man's Fall in Eden, the adversary of God and man channeled all his hellish ingenuity to frustrate God's purpose of grace for mankind.

His slimy trail may be traced throughout the Old Testament, but with the advent of Christ, his assaults became more direct and open. On the cross he launched his final attack against the seed of the woman who was to deal him his deathblow (Genesis 3:15), and at Christ's death it looked as though he had been the victor. But it only seemed so. The Resurrection demonstrated that Christ was victor.

The moment of Satan's triumph was the moment of his defeat. The victim on the cross became the victor through the cross. The joy set before Him (Hebrews 12:2) was already in sight, and now He could gladly summon His servant death and dismiss His spirit.

PART VII: THE WORD OF CONFIDENCE

With awe and reverence we now approach the watershed of the final struggle. The eternal Son of God dismisses His spirit. "Jesus called out with a loud voice, 'Father, into your hands I commit my spirit.' When he had said this, he breathed his last" (Luke 23:46). The body that had housed the Christ was about to be laid in Joseph's tomb, but before He took leave of the earth, Jesus uttered His last word from the cross, and not in subdued tones but with a loud, triumphant voice.

The habits of a lifetime are not easily shaken off. The Master was a man of prayer and a man of the Book. How natural that His last words should blend both characteristics, for this word is at once a prayer and a quotation from the Old Testament: "Into your hands I commit my spirit" (Psalm 31:5). He could not have spoken more appropriately in the moment of His death. He ended His ministry as He began it—with a quotation from Scripture on His lips.

His death was voluntary. In Matthew's account of the Crucifixion (Matthew 27:50), it is stated that He dismissed His spirit. Although from one point of view it is true that His adversaries *did* take His life from Him, it was only by His permission. Before allowing His tormentors to arrest Him, Jesus demonstrated His divine power by causing them to fall backward. But having done this He steadfastly refused to exercise this power to deliver Himself from death. He *chose* death on the cross. He could have saved Himself, but for our sakes He refused to do so.

The bitterest ingredient in the cup of His suffering had been the midnight gloom that enveloped not only His body but also His soul, when His Father made the iniquity of us all to be carried by Him (Isaiah 53:6). Three hours of torture at the hands of His own creatures were succeeded by the infinitely darker three hours into which an eternity of suffering was compressed.

But now He was in the light again. In the midst of His awful abandonment there came the renewed realization of His complete union with His Father. "I and the Father are one" (John 10:30). He does not now cry, "My God, My God!" but, "Father." The communion He had enjoyed from eternity was restored, never again to be interrupted. Small wonder that He cried with a loud and triumphant voice.

Some may question whether Christians sufficiently realize that our Lord's life on earth was a life of moment-by-moment faith and trust in His Father. John's gospel especially reveals the extent of His dependence on His Father. Such characteristic statements as "By myself I can do nothing" (John 5:30) and "The words I say to you are not just my own" (John 14:10) reveal the important part trust played in His relationship with His Father.

Did He trust Him fully in the hour of death? Has His trust been impaired by the awful experience of the cross? Here as at all times He is our example. He shows His disciples in every age how to handle themselves in the hour of death—not yielding to fear but maintaining an attitude of calm, assured confidence.

The secret of our security. Our Lord obviously entertained no thought that death ended existence. He had assured the penitent thief of a place with Him in paradise. Now He speaks as though He was making a deposit in a safe place, to which, after the crisis of death was over, He would come and recover it.

Who would be afraid of death when it means that our spirits are in His hands? How safe and strong they are! "My Father, who has given them [his sheep] to me, is greater than all; no one can snatch them out of my Father's hand" (John 10:29). When we are called upon to face that last enemy, death, let us look on it in the same way as our Lord.

As our Lord closed His eyes in death, His spirit rested in His Father's hands as restfully as a baby on its mother's breast. His final act of self-committal was a simple and genuine act of faith. Nothing more remained to be done. It was completed perfectly according to the divine plan, so by an act of His will He dismissed His spirit. Redemption was completed, awaiting only the Resurrection as God's seal of final acceptance of His Son's sacrifice.

KEY INSIGHT
INTO THE LIFE AND WORK OF CHRIST

In His words of consummation,
even in the midst of great thirst
and other painful needs, Jesus continued
to trust in His Father; expressed faith
in the completed work on the cross, and
committed His destiny into His Father's hands.

26

THE CALVARY
MIRACLES

It was perfectly appropriate that a ministry filled with miracles should conclude with a series of miracles. Jesus was dead and His lips silenced, but now God spoke in an awe-inspiring language of His own. The events attached to His death were startling signs to an unbelieving world and underscored the tremendous significance of the Savior's death.

THE MYSTERIOUS DARKNESS

"Darkness came over the whole land" (Luke 23:44). This was no ordinary darkness. God darkened the sun by His own means. It was not caused by an eclipse. The longest eclipse lasts but a few minutes, but this darkness continued for three hours. Again, it occurred during the Feast of the Passover, the time of full moon, when the moon was at her farthest from the sun.

This unique occurrence has historical support beyond the Bible. In Egypt, when Diogenes saw the darkness, with unconscious insight he exclaimed, "Either the Deity Himself suffers at this moment, or sympathizes with one that does."

In the second century Tertullian challenged his heathen adversaries with the following words, "At the moment of Christ's death, the light departed from the sun, and the land was darkened at noonday, which wonder is related in your own annals, and is preserved in your archives to this day."

This darkness was unique and symbolic. "The darkness was not caused by the absence of the sun, the occasion of our night," wrote W. R. Nicholson. "It was darkness at noon-time, a darkness in the presence of the sun, and while the sun was uneclipsed by the intervention of another celestial body, a darkness we might say, which was the antagonist of light and the overcomer of it. . . . The darkness of Calvary smothering the sun at noon! What an impressive thing! What a trembling conception of the almightiness of God!"

But why this darkness? Because darkness and judgment go together. It assuredly was an awesome sign to the sign-seeking but Christ-rejecting Jews. It was an inspired commentary on the character and extent of His sufferings for us, while He was being "stricken by God, smitten by him, and afflicted" (Isaiah 53:4). Peter, James, and John, intimates of Jesus, were admitted into the secrets of Gethsemane, but at Calvary God enveloped His Son's anguish in a darkness that concealed its full meaning.

The onlookers may well have been struck with fear at God's miraculous intervention. "When all the people who had gathered to witness this sight saw what took place, they beat their breasts and went away" (Luke 23:48).

THE MIRACULOUS RENDING OF THE VEIL

"And, behold, the veil of the temple was rent in twain from the top to the bottom" (Matthew 27:51 KJV). The Holy Place in the temple was divided from the Holiest of All by a great and beautiful veil. It was suspended by hooks from four pillars of gold. It measured sixty feet long by thirty feet wide and was reputed to be as thick as the palm of the hand. It was so heavy that the priests claimed it took three hundred men to handle it.

The purpose of the veil needed no explanation. It was not a gateway but a barrier. It effectively excluded the ministering priests from entering the Holiest of All. Only once a year was it drawn aside to admit the high priest—on the Day of Atonement. He entered the sacred chamber to sprinkle the mercy seat with blood, making atonement for his own sins and those of his people.

For centuries the veil had hung gracefully in its place, but suddenly, at the very moment the Crucified One uttered His loud, expiring cry, the ministering priests heard a tearing sound, and as if an unseen hand severed it by starting at the top, the veil fell apart before their awe-stricken gaze.

Who could express the solemnity of the moment when they found themselves gazing into the sanctuary where for centuries God had chosen to dwell and into which no one had dared to enter under pain of death? Tradition has it that the priests, unwilling to accept the implications of this divine act, sewed up the curtain and resumed their ritual, as though no world-shaking event had taken place.

That this was a miraculous act of God was evident, for the tear was from top to bottom. Some have seen the earthquake that accompanied the rending of the veil as the cause of the phenomenon. One writer suggests that a breakage in the masonry of the porch, which rent the outer veil and left the Holy Place open to view, would account for the language of the Gospels, of Josephus, and of the Talmud. But the thickness of the veil would make that seem most unlikely. That some great catastrophe had occurred in the sanctuary at this very time is confirmed by Tacitus and the earliest Christian tradition, as well as by Josephus and the Talmud. Such a widespread tradition must have a historical basis.

Again, if the earthquake rent a veil of such thickness, why did it not destroy the building at the same time? Be that as it may, it was a deeply significant sign brought about by the hand of God.

The rending of the veil signified the end of the old order and the ushering in of the new. J. Gregory Mantle sees in it a fourfold significance.

It was the end of symbolism. The old economy had fulfilled its purpose and yielded its place to the new. Christ, the great High Priest, was the perfect fulfillment of the shadows and ritual of the Law.

It prefigured the end of sin. The veil was rent at the very moment Jesus, who was "made . . . to be sin for us" (2 Corinthians 5:21), "[did] away with sin by the sacrifice of himself" (Hebrews 9:26).

It was the end of the old sacramental system. No longer was there any need for a priesthood and a sacrificial system. The ministration of the priesthood that had held a central place in Jewish national life had come to an end.

It symbolized the end of separation. The veil that had for a millennium and a half been a barrier to God's presence now became a gateway. Every penitent soul is now invited to enter the Holiest of All by virtue of the blood of Jesus (Hebrews 10:19).

THE MIGHTY EARTHQUAKE

Our Lord's victorious shout was followed immediately by a shattering earthquake. The rocks that split were not detached boulders, but cliffs —masses of rock. Earthquake shocks are not uncommon in Jerusalem, but through divine overruling this particular quake synchronized with the tremendous event that had just transpired in the spiritual realm, as though to attest the might and majesty of Him whose lifeless body now hung limp on the cross.

This was no small earth tremor, because the rocks split and were not merely lined with just perceptible cracks but wrenched apart into such gulfs as to lay open the interior of the rocky graves which abounded in Golgotha. The event was of such great magnitude that even the Roman soldiers "were terrified" (Matthew 27:54).

This was not an isolated phenomenon due to natural causes. The coincidences are too striking. It exactly coincided with two other miraculous manifestations, the mysterious darkness and the rending of the veil. It occurred together with the loud cry and the death of the Son of God. It also coincided with the opening of certain graves, apparently only the graves of godly people.

Some have seen in this divine visitation an answer to the earthquake on Sinai that demonstrated the awesome presence of God. In the Old

Testament, an earthquake often denoted God's presence and intervention among His creatures. "Sinai was the prophecy of Calvary. Calvary was the fulfillment of Sinai. Sinai was God's unchangeable voice of condemnation; Calvary, God's Fatherly voice of pardon and love."

THE MOMENTOUS
APPEARANCE OF DEAD SAINTS

"The tombs broke open and the bodies of many holy people who had died were raised to life. They came out of the tombs, and after Jesus' resurrection they went into the holy city and appeared to many people" (Matthew 27:52–53).

The earthquake shock and the splitting of the rocks resulted in the opening of the rock-tombs similar to that of Joseph of Arimathea, in the vicinity of Calvary. It was not blind force that split the rocks. They were split in a careful way, for there was every evidence of intelligent design. Only selected graves were opened, the graves of godly people. There is no evidence that graves other than those were breached by the quake.

The Persic version reads, "Saints who had suffered martyrdom rose," and Matthew Henry asks, "What if we should suppose that they were the martyrs who, in Old Testament times had sealed the truth of God with their blood, that were thus dignified and distinguished?"

It must be noted that, while the tombs were opened at the moment of Christ's death, the bodies of the saints are recorded to have come "out of the graves *after* his resurrection" (Matthew 27:53 KJV). The tombs thus remained exposed for the period the body of Christ remained in the grave. The later appearance of the saints would be all the more striking and significant, showing as it did the "better resurrection" yet to come, of which Christ was the firstfruits.

The opening of the tombs was a vivid and eloquent symbolic demonstration that by His death Christ had forever broken the bonds of death. "He death by dying slew" and forever robbed the grave of its terror and victory.

The resurrection of these saints was a clear indication that the prison doors of Hades had been wrenched from their hinges. The words "many holy people . . . were raised" surely mean what they say. They rose, but not in order that they might live again on earth. They "appeared to many people," but not to stay on earth.

Our Lord's own resurrection is no more miraculous than the mysterious darkness and the rending of the veil, which we have already discussed. It gives point to the opening of the tombs, for the saints who appeared were not "risen" saints but "revived" saints, as was Lazarus when called back to life. Their bodies were apparently revived for this purpose, but this was not their final resurrection.

We have a sign in this momentous event that Jesus had conquered death, and a foreshadowing of the glorious resurrection that awaits the believer.

KEY INSIGHT
INTO THE LIFE AND WORK OF CHRIST

In the signs following His death, Christ demonstrated both that the Old Testament sacrifices had become obsolete and also that He had defeated the power of death.

27

THE RESURRECTION
OF CHRIST

Does it matter very much whether or not Christ rose from the dead? To read Paul's letters will leave us in no doubt as to the centrality of this major doctrine of our faith.

"If Christ has not been raised, our preaching is useless and so is your faith. More than that, we are then found to be false witnesses about God. . . . And if Christ has not been raised, your faith is futile; you are still in your sins. Then those who have fallen asleep in Christ are lost. If only in this life we have hope in Christ, we are to be pitied more than all men" (1 Corinthians 15:14–15, 17–19).

The doctrine of the Resurrection is central in the Christian faith, not peripheral. To deny it is to remove the keystone of the arch of Christianity. Without it, the crucifixion of our Lord would have been in vain, for it was the Resurrection that validated the atoning death of Christ.

Of all the great religions, Christianity alone bases its claim to acceptance on the resurrection of its Founder. If it is not a fact, our preaching is emptied of content. Instead of being a dynamic message of a person who exists forever, it merely enshrines a fragrant memory of a person long gone. Our faith is without a factual basis and is therefore empty. The Scripture writers become purveyors of intentional lies and the Scriptures themselves unreliable. Deliverance from the penalty and power of sin is no more than a mirage, and the future life is still shrouded in total darkness.

If this doctrine means much to the believer, it is no less important to the Lord Himself. If the Resurrection can be disproved, He is forever discredited as Redeemer and Son of God, for He frequently appealed to His future resurrection as evidence of the truth of His claims: "As Jonah was three days and three nights in the belly of a huge fish, so the Son of Man will be three days and three nights in the heart of the earth" (Matthew 12:40).

DENIALS AND ERRONEOUS EXPLANATIONS

It would appear that attempts to explain away the physical resurrection of Christ or to deny its factuality have their rise more in unbelief of the supernatural than in an objective examination of the evidence for it. In this connection, W. Graham Scroggie wrote: "The resurrection is not denied because the evidence is regarded as insufficient, but the evidence is rejected and repudiated because the resurrection is denied. A resurrection is regarded as impossible and little attempt is made to explain away the evidence on which it rests. But the improbability of supernaturalism is one of the most arrogant assumptions ever made. It takes for granted what still needs to be proved. Such a method is utterly unscientific. The true scientific method is to examine the facts and then form a theory; not first to form a theory and then flout and repudiate and deny the facts."

Bultmann's attitude to the Resurrection bears this out. "A corpse cannot come to life again and climb out of the grave," he wrote, beginning with an assumption that yet remains to be proved. "It is quite possible to speak of a resurrection," he continued, "but Jesus was not raised to a new life; rather, He rose into the *kerygma*. That is, there is no living Christ who is a divine person, he is present only where the Word that testifies of Him is proclaimed."

It is only to be expected that the archenemy of God and man would do all in his power to discredit this event, which inflicted such disastrous defeat on him. The denials began the very day He rose and have recurred periodically ever since. The plain fact was that the tomb was empty. How could such a conclusive piece of evidence be explained away?

The chief priests' explanation was simple. The disciples themselves removed the body and then pretended He had risen (Matthew 27:63–64).

Although the disciples did not grasp the full meaning of His predictions of resurrection (John 20:9), it was perfectly clear to His enemies, who took pains to guard against a faked resurrection by sealing the tomb and posting a guard at the spot. "[They] stole him away while we were asleep," the soldiers were told to testify (Matthew 28:13; see also v. 15). But the testimony of sleeping witnesses to what took place during their slumbers is hardly acceptable. If the disciples had indeed stolen the body, why would they be willing to experience torture and death for what they knew was a lie?

The unbeliever's attitude is at least honest. He just flatly denies the fact and possibility of resurrection. "I would not believe Jesus rose, even if I saw it," declared Ernest Renan. This statement accords perfectly with our Lord's words: "If they do not listen to Moses and the Prophets, they will not be convinced even if someone rise from the dead" (Luke 16:31). And yet those who shrink back from the miracle of resurrection often accept without question the mysteries of nature, compared with which, Huxley says, the mysteries of the Bible are child's play.

The problem of discrepancies. That it is difficult to harmonize all the details of the recorded appearances of our Lord is granted. But as one writer puts it, one would not deny that the sun had risen because of discrepancies among observers.

Actually, the apparent discrepancies argue rather for the truthfulness of the narrative, for they are evidence that the writers have not tried to obtain artificial agreement on every detail, as they might easily have done. And if we knew all, might we not be able to harmonize it all?

Was it only a swoon? Crucifixion is a slow death, and victims have been known to live three days on the cross, whereas Jesus hung there for only a few hours. It is suggested that the supposed death was only a swoon, from which He recovered when placed in the cool air of the tomb, amid the fragrant spices.

Consider the following facts against this view. The centurion, experienced in crucifixions, gave a death certificate (John 19:33). Christ's body was pierced by the soldier's spear, and blood and water gushed out. His crucifixion had been preceded by the agony in the garden and the merciless scourging that had so exhausted Him that He staggered under the weight of the cross.

Think, too, of the obstacles to His escape from the tomb: the sealed door, the guards, the huge stone to be removed. Would someone who had experienced the ordeal of scourging and crucifixion appear to His disciples as a radiant and healthy conqueror? Even David Strauss, who vigorously opposed the teaching of Christ's resurrection, was compelled in honesty to write: "It is impossible that one who had just come forth from the grave half-dead, who crept about weak and ill, who stood in need of medical treatment and bandaging, strengthening and tender care, and who at last succumbed to suffering, could ever have given to the disciples the impression that He was a conqueror over death and the grave and that He was the Prince of Life."

Was the tomb mistaken? It has been suggested that the women went to the wrong tomb because their eyes were blinded with tears. This is most unlikely, for the women had been present at the entombment on Friday and had observed the tomb. If the women mistook the tomb, then Peter and John must also have mistaken it. Jesus was buried in a private garden, not in a public burial ground where such a mistake might be easy.

Was it a hallucination? Did the excitement of the disciples bring about hallucinations? Did they only *think* they saw Jesus because they were already persuaded He was alive?

No, for His resurrection was the last thing they expected. It was a dead Christ whom the women went to embalm. To the last person, the disciples were slow to believe. The law of hallucinations is that they increase in frequency and intensity, but in this case they decreased and shortly ceased entirely. Jesus appeared at least ten times in forty days, and then His appearances ceased as abruptly as they had begun. And did all the "five hundred . . . brothers" to whom he appeared "at the same time" (1 Corinthians 15:6) have the same hallucination? Surely this is far-fetched.

It is noteworthy that none of these supposed explanations is accepted generally today by those who deny the Resurrection. No single one has ever gained general and lasting approval. Indeed no theory has yet been put forth on which opposers of the supernatural have all agreed.

THE TRUE EXPLANATION

We are forced back to the simple conclusion that fits all the facts and agrees with all the records—the body of Christ was actually raised from the dead. His was no mere "spiritual resurrection," nor were His appearances mere spiritual manifestations (Luke 24:36–43).

He appeared in His resurrection body, not in the dusk but in lighted rooms in the light of day, visible and tangible. He appeared in the same body in which He had been entombed but possessed new characteristics. It was easily recognizable but could become unrecognizable or invisible at will (John 20:14–15; 21:4, 12). It transcended the laws of matter and experienced no interference from closed doors (John 20:26). Unlike that of Lazarus, who was raised to die again, the body of Jesus was immortal (Romans 6:9–10).

With Paul we can cry with glad assurance, "Christ has indeed been raised from the dead" (1 Corinthians 15:20).

THE RESURRECTION APPEARANCES

As has been stated, it is not easy to reconcile the records of the appearances of our Lord, but there were at least ten, and there may have been as many as thirteen if the appearances to Paul and Stephen are included. They were not all on one day but extended over forty days.

To Mary Magdalene (John 20:14–16; Mark 16:9–11)

To other women (Matthew 28:8–10)

To Peter (Luke 24:34; 1 Corinthians 15:5)

To the Emmaus disciples (Luke 24:13–31; Mark 16:12–13)
To the ten (Luke 24:36; John 20:19)
To the eleven (Mark 16:14; John 20:26; 1 Corinthians 15:5)
To the seven (John 21:1–14)
On the Galilee mountain (Matthew 28:16–17; Mark 16:15–18)
To the five hundred (1 Corinthians 15:6)
To James (1 Corinthians 15:7)
At the Ascension (Luke 24:44–53; Mark 16:19–20; Acts 1:6–11)
To Stephen (Acts 7:56)
To Paul (1 Corinthians 15:8)

EVIDENCE FOR THE RESURRECTION

The manner in which the event is recorded bears evidence of its truth. Exaggeration is avoided, and the blindness and ignorance of the disciples are straightforwardly recorded. Referring to the records, H. C. G. Moule wrote, "These unexplained details, just because they are unexplained, coming one after another as they do, set down so simply and without anxiety, yet minutely, carry the very tone and accent of eyewitnesses. We seem to stand there watching; the whole motion of the scene is before us. All is near, real, natural, visible."

The life of Christ demands such a climax. If we believe He was supernaturally conceived, lived without sin, died a voluntary, atoning death, then the Resurrection is easy to believe. Without it, a perfect life would end in a shameful death, surely an inappropriate close. The Resurrection cannot be isolated from all that preceded it.

The empty grave and the disappearance of the body argue it (Matthew 28:6). Karl Barth wrote: "We must not transmute the resurrection into a spiritual event. We must listen to it and let it tell us the story how there was an empty grave, that new life beyond the grave did become visible."

There can only be two alternatives. The body was removed by either human or divine hands, for there is no doubt the tomb was empty on the first Easter morning. The former must have been the hands of friends or of foes. The foes *would* not, and the friends *could* not remove it. In any case His friends did not expect Him to rise. Why did the Jews not produce the body if it was not raised, and thus silence His disciples forever? To produce the body would be the end of Christianity, for "the Church of Christ is built on an empty tomb."

The dramatic transformation of the disciples attested to it. A sudden change in people is a psychological fact that demands explanation. How can the radical change in the disciples be accounted for? After the death of their leader they were a demoralized band of men, plunged in despair. They had lost faith in their cause. Shortly afterward they were again a united band, zealous for their cause, willing to suffer imprisonment and even death for it. What produced this dramatic change? Overnight skeptics became ardent witnesses who never again yielded to doubt. Why, if not because Jesus did really appear to them?

The very existence of the church is tangible evidence. What brought into existence the first Christian community? It has been well said that Christianity died with Christ and was laid with Him in the tomb. The Resurrection was accompanied by the indisputable resurrection of Christianity. Within fifty days of its occurrence, Peter was preaching the Resurrection with great power and effect, and thereafter it became the most prominent theme of apostolic witness. If the risen Christ had not appeared to them, there would never have been a Christian church. This primitive belief is inexplicable if the Resurrection is not a fact. Within twenty-five years of the event it was accepted as a fact by the whole church and in places as far removed from one another as Jerusalem and Rome. The early church did not manufacture the resurrection belief; the Resurrection created the church.

The witness of Paul confirms it. Is it credible that a man of Paul's mental abilities and education, a man who had been a violent persecutor of the church, should have come to believe the Resurrection absolutely irrefutable if in reality it was not a fact? It was the fact that he had actually seen the Lord in His risen body that provided the inspiration and motivation of his service.

The Lord's Day stems from the Resurrection. From where did this revolutionary idea derive? What caused Jewish believers, schooled in the Sabbath tradition, to abandon the Jewish sabbath and instead observe the

Lord's Day? How did the day come to be changed, not by decree but by common consent? The event that brought about this stupendous and revolutionary change was the resurrection of our Lord from the dead. The Lord's Day is the effect. The Resurrection is the cause. As early as A.D. 70, Barnabas, one of the early Fathers, wrote: "We keep the Lord's Day with joyfulness, the day also on which Jesus rose from the dead."

KEY INSIGHT
INTO THE LIFE AND WORK OF CHRIST

The resurrection of Christ is the central teaching of Christianity that elevates it above all other religions, and there is strong evidence to support a literal and bodily resurrection of Christ.

28

THE MINISTRY
OF THE FORTY DAYS

The activities of our Lord during the period between His resurrection and His ascension are not always given the place of importance they deserve. It is not difficult to imagine how thrilling it must have been to the dispirited disciples to speak with their risen Master, to listen again to that familiar voice. The topics of their discussion are summed up in the phrase "things pertaining to the kingdom of God" (Acts 1:3 KJV).

Apart from the incidents recorded in the Gospels, the only fragment of His teaching during this transitional period preserved to us is contained in Acts 1:1–8. But a careful study of this paragraph in conjunction with the relevant passages in the Gospels provides illuminating insight into the significance of those days.

The Christ whose life was lived, whose service was performed, and whose death was achieved "through the eternal Spirit" (Hebrews 9:14), even after His resurrection, gave commandments to His followers "through the Holy Spirit" (Acts 1:2). Here was admirable evidence of the harmony and interdependence of members of the Godhead as they worked together for our redemption and sanctification.

AN EVIDENTIAL VALUE

His primary objective was doubtless to provide His disciples with incontrovertible evidence that death had not held Him as its prey. "He shewed himself alive after his passion by many infallible proofs" (Acts 1:3 KJV). He lingered long enough on earth to prove to His followers the truth of His resurrection, and they were not easily convinced. They had been "slow of heart to believe" (Luke 24:25) that the tomb was indeed empty, so He provided them with impressive proof of His survival.

The phrase "many infallible proofs" signifies the strongest proof of which a subject is capable. The very fact that the disciples were not in the least gullible and had to have their doubts thoroughly removed is in itself proof of the most convincing kind that Jesus did rise and appear to them as Scripture records. And they were so completely convinced that they never doubted again.

Although it was at great cost and often against their personal interest, they bore courageous testimony to the Resurrection, simply because their experience and observation compelled them to do so. He presented them with the signs of bodily identity in the scars in hands and feet and side—an evidence of identity that would be accepted in any court of law (John 20:27).

AN EXPLANATORY VALUE

The passage in Acts 1:1–8 is obviously a greatly condensed summary of Jesus' instructions to the men to whom He was entrusting the evangelization of the world. His conversation must have covered a very wide field, and Luke, guided by the Spirit, has preserved for us some of the more important themes around which His teaching revolved.

He gave a hint as to the nature of His kingdom (Acts 1:3, 6–7). His appearances, disappearances, and reappearances were designed to impress on them the fact that His kingdom was "not of this world" (John 18:36). They were anticipating a nationalistic kingdom of earthly glory. "Lord, are you at this time going to restore the kingdom to Israel?" (Acts 1:6).

Jesus wanted them to learn that from now on their relationship with Him would be entirely on a spiritual basis. They must divest themselves of the idea of an immediate defeat of Rome and establishment of a Jewish kingdom. The timing of that event was God's concern, not theirs (Acts 1:7).

He indicated the nature of the apostolic mission. "Ye shall be witnesses unto me both in Jerusalem, and in all Judaea, and in Samaria and unto the uttermost part of the earth" (Acts 1:8 KJV). His program was clearly defined and explicit. The word of their witness was to extend from Jerusalem as the center in ever-widening circles until it had reached earth's remotest boundaries. It should be noted that our Lord did not say, "*First* Jerusalem, *then* Judea and *then* Samaria," but "*both* Jerusalem *and* Judea *and* Samaria *and* the uttermost part of the earth." They were not selfishly to hug their own spiritual privileges and blessings.

He revealed to them the source of their power for such a stupendous, mind-stretching enterprise. As He unfolded His plan, they might well have protested, "Who is equal to such a task?" (2 Corinthians 2:16). He revealed to them the source of their power beforehand: "Stay in the city [of Jerusalem] until you have been clothed with power from on high" (Luke 24:49). He reminded them again of His provision: "You will receive power when the Holy Spirit comes on you" (Acts 1:8). He was not going to leave them dependent on merely human resources for what was clearly a superhuman task.

AN EVANGELISTIC VALUE

Most of our Lord's post-Resurrection appearances had some relation to the extension of His kingdom. He desired to infuse His followers with the missionary passion that blazed at white heat in His own breast. The enterprise to which He was calling them extended to every nation, every community, every creature in the whole world (Matthew 28:19).

Notice the keynote of His conversations with His disciples. When He appeared *to the ten,* His commission was, "As the Father has sent me, I am sending you" (John 20:21). He invested them with the same authority as He had received from the Father. They were to be missionaries under His orders, even as He had been a missionary under His Father's direction. In the same interview He banished their fears by bestowing His peace and imparted to them the Holy Spirit.

To the seven on the sea of Tiberias (John 21:1–2) He gave the symbolic command to those whom He had said were to become fishers of men, "Throw your net on the right side of the boat and you will find some," thus teaching them that only as much of their service as was Christ-directed would be successful in taking men alive for the kingdom. At the same time He instructed Peter—and the others as well—in the art of feeding both the sheep and the lambs of the flock.

To the disciples on the mountain in Galilee (Matthew 28:16–20) Jesus outlined His program of world evangelization. "Therefore go and make disciples of all nations, . . . teaching them to obey everything I have commanded you. And surely I am with you always, to the very end of the age." Here was a command both universal and individual, binding on all His followers in all ages.

To the eleven at Jerusalem (Luke 24:44–53) Jesus commanded that "repentance and forgiveness of sins will be preached in his name to all nations, beginning at Jerusalem. You are witnesses of these things." He followed this at once with the command to wait in Jerusalem until they had received the expression of power that alone would enable them to handle the staggering commission He had given them.

So on each occasion when He met His disciples, the great burden of His heart found expression. Only by their loving obedience could they enable Him to "see of the travail of his soul, and . . . be satisfied" (Isaiah 53:11 KJV).

The matters of which Jesus made no mention are equally striking and significant in our materialistic and computerized age. The financial problems that loom so largely in our calculations were not even mentioned. Methods of organization, structure of the church, and type of church buildings were alike ignored. But great emphasis was laid upon utter and absolute abandonment to His leading and devotion to His person as the motive power of evangelistic endeavor.

AN ESCHATOLOGICAL VALUE

Throughout all our Lord's conversations there was the underlying assumption that this evangelistic thrust was not to continue forever. It would lead to a glorious consummation. "Until I return" was the time factor that Jesus used in speaking to Peter (John 21:22–23). He promised His presence "to the very end [or consummation] of the age" (Matthew 28:20).

Those statements limited the scope of evangelistic opportunity to the period between our Lord's ascension and His second advent. Since that is so, we should seize with both hands such opportunities of reaching "every creature" in our generation as still remain.

KEY INSIGHT
INTO THE LIFE AND WORK OF CHRIST

During the forty days of post-Resurrection ministry, Jesus revealed more of the nature of His kingdom as well as the need to gather in people from all over the world.

29

THE ASCENSION
OF CHRIST

W hen he had led them out to the vicinity of Bethany, he lifted up
his hands and blessed them. While he was blessing them, he left
them and was taken up into heaven" (Luke 24:50–51).

The story of the ascension of Christ is specifically described only
three times. Luke records it twice. With simple brevity Mark wrote, "After the Lord Jesus had spoken to them, he was taken up into heaven and
he sat at the right hand of God" (Mark 16:19). Luke adds a further touch
in addition to the words at the head of this chapter, "After he said this,
he was taken up before their very eyes, and a cloud hid him from their
sight" (Acts 1:9). Although these are the only detailed references to the
episode, eleven other New Testament books make reference to it.

This crowning event was not without previous foreshadowing. Jesus
Himself had clearly predicted it when He said, "What if you see the
Son of Man ascend to where he was before!" (John 6:62) or again, "I go
to the one who sent me" (John 7:33). The psalmist had written antici-
patively, "Thou hast ascended on high . . . : thou hast received gifts for
men" (Psalm 68:18 KJV), a passage that Paul applies to Christ (Ephesians 4:8).

It is a matter of surprise that so small a body of literature centers on
this amazing and important event, especially as it has such far-reaching

implications for the Christian. W. H. Griffith Thomas rightly claims that the Ascension is not only a great historical fact of the New Testament but a great factor in the life of Christ and Christians, since it is the consummation of His redemptive work.

The Ascension was closely linked to, and the logical outcome of, the Resurrection. No more fitting climax could have been conceived for such a life as Christ lived. When He ascended, not a claim of God on mankind was left unsettled and not a promise left in uncertainty. The spectacular method of His departure from earth was entirely consistent with the miraculous achievements of His life and work.

THE MANNER OF THE ASCENSION

It was of tremendous importance that our Lord's final departure from earth should not be a mere vanishing out of their sight, as He did at Emmaus. This would result in uncertainty as to whether or not He might again appear. Accordingly, the Ascension took place not at night but in broad daylight. While "they were looking intently up into the sky" He rose from their midst, not because He must do so to go to His Father but in order to make the act symbolic and understandable to them.

Significantly, it was not at Bethlehem, or at the Transfiguration mount, or even at Calvary that the event took place, but at Bethany, the place of His sweetest earthly fellowship.

This appearance and disappearance of the risen Christ is represented as an episode as real and objective as His other appearances during the forty days. Those appearances were calculated to assure His disciples that He had conquered death and hell and was recognized as God's Messiah. The Ascension was intended to convince them that they need not expect Him to appear again. No other mode of departure would have left the same impression. The period of transition had ended, and they need no longer remain in suspense. He left His own in the very act of blessing. For this He had come, and He blessed them as He departed, not as a condemning judge but as a compassionate friend and High Priest, with hands outstretched.

THE NECESSITY FOR THE ASCENSION

An ascension such as the Gospels record was essential for a number of reasons. It is not a marginal doctrine of Scripture. As J. C. Davies puts it, "If it is through the ascension that Jesus entered upon the office of Son of Man, became no longer *Messiah designatus* but Messiah indeed, and received the regal dignity and title of 'Lord,' then the ascension belongs not to the periphery, but to the heart and substance of the gospel."

It was essential for the following reasons, among others.

The nature of our Lord's resurrection body necessitated it. Such a body would not be permanently at home on earth. He must depart, but by glorification rather than by mortal corruption.

The unique personality and holy life of our Lord demanded an exit from this world as remarkable and fitting as His entrance into it. If a miraculous exit was granted to sinful men such as Enoch and Elijah, how much more to the sinless Son of God?

His redemptive work required such a departure. Without it, His work would have remained incomplete for it rests on four pillars—the Incarnation, Crucifixion, Resurrection, and Ascension. The Ascension was a complete and final demonstration that His atonement had forever solved the problem created by man's sin and rebellion. Only in this way could He be rightfully called Head of the church (Ephesians 1:19–23).

The gift of the Holy Spirit was dependent on His glorification. "Up to that time the Spirit had not been given, since Jesus had not yet been glorified" was John's comment on the Lord's promise of the Spirit (John 7:39).

It enabled the disciples to give to the world *a satisfactory account of the disappearance of Christ's body from the tomb.*

To question the historicity of the Ascension would be to put the whole drama of redemption into the realm of doubt.

THE SIGNIFICANCE OF
THE ASCENSION FOR CHRIST HIMSELF

To Him the Ascension came as *the culminating divine assurance* that the work He had come to do had been completed to the entire satisfaction of the Father, to whose right hand He had now been exalted. "The right hand of God" is metaphorical language for divine omnipotence. "Sitting" does not imply that He is resting but rather that He is reigning as King and exercising divine omnipotence. The doctrine of the Ascension is therefore the divine affirmation of the absolute sovereignty of Christ over the whole universe. "There is no sphere, however secular," says B. M. Metzger, "in which Christ has no rights—and no sphere in which His servants are absolved from obedience to Him."

It was *a divine vindication of His claims to deity* that had been rejected by the Jews. He had claimed the right to ascend into heaven as His own prerogative. "No one has ever gone into heaven except the one who came from heaven—the Son of Man" (John 3:13). From that point on He can exercise those prerogatives and dignities that He laid aside for our salvation.

Finally, it was *His divine inauguration into His heavenly priesthood,* a subject treated in another chapter.

For the believer, our Lord's ascension has blessed implications for us. Though physically remote, He is always spiritually near. Now free from earthly limitations, His life above is both the promise and the guarantee of ours. "Because I live, you also will live," He assured His disciples (John 14:19). His ascension anticipates our glorification and leaves us the assurance that He has gone to prepare a place for us (John 14:2).

His resurrection and ascension to heaven involved nothing less than the making of His humanity eternal in a transfigured and glorified form, even if it may be wholly incomprehensible to us. It brings Him very near to us as we remember that He carried His humanity back with Him to heaven (Hebrews 2:14–18).

"He led captivity captive" (Ephesians 4:8 KJV). His ascension was His triumphant return to heaven and indicated that the tyrannical reign of sin was ended.

"The ascension helped to clarify the nature of the Messiahship to the apostles," writes R. H. Laver. "They expected a Davidic king, whereas the crucifixion presented them with a suffering Servant. Then the resurrection proclaimed a king after all. The ascension further clarified the nature of His Kingship. The Kingdom of Christ is indeed not of this world. He will reign, but it shall not be simply from an earthly throne. His Kingdom will be glorious but it shall not be achieved through the blood and steel of men. The Cross was the decisive and atoning conflict; the resurrection was the proclamation of triumph; the ascension was the Conqueror's return with the captives of war which issued in the enthronement of the victorious King."

KEY INSIGHT
INTO THE LIFE AND WORK OF CHRIST

Christ's ascension presupposes our own glorification and draws us closer to Him as we realize that He carried His humanity back to heaven.

THE HIGH PRIESTLY
MINISTRY OF CHRIST

From the dawn of human history humans have craved a priest, or mediator, who would represent them to God. Among us there is a universal sense that there is a God who has been offended by man's wrongdoing and must be appeased. From our earliest days an instinctive feeling has been expressed that the one who can do this must be someone capable of compassion for human frailty and yet who possesses special influence with God. The patriarch Job lamented, "There is no umpire between us, who might lay his hand upon us both" (Job 9:33 RSV).

This universal desire resulted in the creation of orders of priests who, men ardently hoped, would be able to mediate with God on their behalf. Human priesthood reached its zenith in Judaism, but the story of the Jewish priesthood only serves to reveal how tragically it failed those who pinned their hopes to it. It is only in Christ, the ideal High Priest, that this deep and hidden yearning of the human heart finds complete fulfillment.

CHRIST'S QUALIFICATIONS AS HIGH PRIEST

The writer to the Hebrews clearly sets out the necessary qualifications for a Jewish high priest. "Every high priest is selected from among men and is appointed to represent them in matters related to God, to offer gifts and sacrifices for sins. He is able to deal gently with those who are ignorant and are going astray, since he himself is subject to weakness" (Hebrews 5:1–2).

Two great essentials will be noted.

Fellowship with others. He must be linked to other men by the ties of a common humanity. He must be "selected from among men." In no other way would he be "able to deal gently" with those whom he was to represent. The idea behind the words "deal gently with" has been expressed as "able to have a moderate attitude toward" the ignorant. That is, he would be neither too lenient nor too severe. Sympathy and compassion are of the essence of the priesthood.

But merely human qualities were not sufficient for an office that demanded so delicate and demanding a relationship. There must also be *authority from God.* The high priest must be "appointed to act on behalf of men in relation to God" (Hebrews 5:1 RSV). He cannot be self-appointed. "No man taketh this honor unto himself" (Hebrews 5:4 ASV). His is a divine appointment.

Does Christ satisfy these requirements? Indeed He does. In order to help the race of which He had become part, He was made "like his brothers in every way, in order that he might become a merciful and faithful high priest in service to God" (Hebrews 2:17). And in order that this identification might be complete, He came not as a king but as a mere working man. He experienced the pinch of poverty and the grip of care. He knew the heights of popularity and the depths of rejection.

He also received His authority from God. "So Christ also did not take upon himself the glory of becoming a high priest. But God said to him, 'You are my Son; today I have become your Father'" (Hebrews 5:5). He was not self-elected but God-appointed.

Further, He was morally and spiritually qualified to exercise this ministry. The High Priest who "always lives to intercede" for us is "holy, blameless, pure, set apart from sinners, exalted above the heavens" (Hebrews 7:25–26). He faithfully fulfilled His whole duty to God. He was entirely without deception in His character. He was stainlessly pure.

Although experiencing the full blast of human temptation, He was morally separate from human sin. Because He conquered temptation and emerged sinless, He was exalted to the right hand of God.

HIS CAPABILITIES AS HIGH PRIEST

Three statements are made in the Hebrews letter in this connection. *He is able to meet our needs.* "Because he himself suffered when he was tempted, he is able to help those who are being tempted" (Hebrews 2:18). Because He was truly man, our Lord was able to meet us on the plane of our human needs. We are willing to aid those requiring help, but too often we have to mourn our inability to do so. Our High Priest knows no such limitations. It should be noted that Christ's ability to aid the tempted is grounded not in mere *pity,* but in costly *reconciliation.* "It behoved him . . . to make reconciliation [propitiation or expiation] for the sins of the people" (Hebrews 2:17 KJV). It is because He thus suffered that He is able to aid us.

He is able to sympathize. "We have not a high priest who is unable to sympathize with our weaknesses, but one who in every respect has been tempted as we are, yet without sin" (Hebrews 4:15 RSV). He never condones or sympathizes with our sin, only with our weaknesses. He always condemns sin because it brings on judgment and breaks fellowship with God. As our advocate He keeps open the way of restoration of lost fellowship upon repentance and confession. Because He has borne the penalty and exhausted the judgment of our sin, He is able to cleanse us on sincere confession of sin (1 John 1:9).

He sympathizes with our weaknesses. Sympathy is the ability to enter into the experiences of another as if they were one's own, and sympathy is deepest when one has suffered the same experience. Christ was "in every respect . . . tempted as we are." He felt the grueling pressure of sin on every part of His nature, yet He emerged without yielding to its seduction. He is thus able to enter sympathetically into the suffering of those passing through the fires of testing.

He is able to save. "He is able to save completely those who come to

God through him, because he always lives to intercede for them" (Hebrews 7:25). Since He lives forever as our mediator and High Priest, He is "able to bring to final completion the salvation of all who draw near to God," as it has been put. The present tense is used in Hebrews 7:25, signifying "a sustained experience resulting from a continuous practice." Thus, "He is able to keep on saving those who are continually coming to God by Him."

Our High Priest is able to save us completely. There is no personal problem for which He has no solution, no enemy from whom He cannot rescue us, no sin from which He cannot deliver us—because He ever lives to make intercession for us.

HIS INTERCESSION AS HIGH PRIEST

Since the writer to the Hebrews assures us that He is "Jesus Christ . . . the same yesterday and today and forever" (Hebrews 13:8), we can gain some light on this subject from His intercession when on earth. It will be noted that most of our Lord's recorded prayers were intercessory —offered on behalf of others. On only one occasion did He assert His own will, and then it was that His loved people should share His glory (John 17:24).

Two words are used of our Lord's ministry of intercession. The first refers to rescue by someone who happens upon another in need and then helps without being asked. Our Lord's prayer for Peter is an illustration. Unknown to himself, Peter was about to face a tremendous spiritual crisis. His omniscient Lord knew it, however, and in the presence of His disciples said, "Simon, Simon, behold, Satan hath desired to have *you*"— plural, all you disciples—"but I have prayed for *thee*"—singular—"that thy faith fail not" (Luke 22:31–32 KJV, italics added). This was unsought intercession that saw a need of which the person was unaware. In the event, Peter failed the test, but his faith did not fail.

The second word, "advocate" (1 John 2:1 KJV; "one who speaks . . . in our defense," NIV), means one who comes to help in response to a call of need or danger, one who pleads our cause and restores us. So whether our need is conscious or unconscious, we have a great High Priest who "lives to make intercession for us."

THE MODE OF HIS INTERCESSION

Our idea of intercession is often associated with agonized pleading or tearful supplication. It is sometimes wrongly conceived as an attempt to overcome the reluctance of God. But our High Priest does not appear as seeker before a God who has to be coaxed into granting a divine blessing. Christ appears as our advocate, not to appeal for clemency but to claim justice for us—to claim what we are entitled to in virtue of His sacrifice on Calvary. He obtains this for us from a God who is "faithful and just and will forgive us our sins" (1 John 1:9).

His intercession is not an audible saying of prayers. When Aaron, the first Jewish high priest, made his annual appearance in the Holiest of All in the tabernacle, he never uttered a word. The silence of the sanctuary was broken only by the tinkling of the golden bells on his garment. It was the blood he bore that spoke, not Aaron himself (Leviticus 16:12–16). It is the presence of our intercessor before the throne, bearing in His body the evidence of His suffering and victory, that speaks for us.

The story is told of Amintas, a Greek soldier who was to be tried for treason. When his brother Aeschylus, who had lost an arm in the service of his country, heard this, he hastened to the court. As sentence was about to be passed, he intervened and holding up the stump of his arm cried, "Amintas is guilty, but for Aeschylus's sake he shall go free." Even so does our High Priest and intercessor intervene on our behalf.

His intercession is personal. "He always lives to intercede for them" (Hebrews 7:25, italics added). It is His personal responsibility, which He does not delegate to angels or men. He is never so preoccupied as to be unable to care for our concerns. As on earth, so in heaven He is still One who serves His creatures.

His intercession is forever. "He *always* lives to intercede for them." He died on the cross to obtain salvation for us. On the throne He lives to maintain us in salvation. It is in this sense that "we [shall] be saved through his [risen] life" (Romans 5:10). We could not live the Christian life for a day were it not that He lives to intercede for us.

He receives and presents our prayers. How can our consciously imperfect prayers be acceptable to our holy God? Our High Priest receives our prayers and mingles with them the incense of His own merits. "Another angel, who had a golden censer, came and stood at the altar. He was given much incense to offer, with the prayers of all the saints, on the golden altar before the throne" (Revelation 8:3).

Every prayer of faith presented by the Son, who is always in harmony with the will and purposes of His Father, becomes His own prayer and meets with the acceptance accorded to Him. Our prayers do not ascend alone but are steeped in His merits, and His intercession is always prevailing.

In view of all that precedes, it is small wonder that the writer of the Hebrews letter sums up the high priestly ministry of Christ in these words: "Now of the things which we have spoken this is the sum: *We have such an high priest,* who is set on the right hand of the throne of the Majesty in the heavens" (Hebrews 8:1 KJV, italics added).

KEY INSIGHT
INTO THE LIFE AND WORK OF CHRIST

Because of His identification with us, Christ is able to sympathize with us, but better yet, to save us completely through His intercession.

THE SECOND
ADVENT OF CHRIST

O f all the notable events enacted on the stage of this world from
Creation onwards, the most remarkable and glorious is yet to come.
Among the inspired prophetic descriptions of that momentous event
are these vivid word pictures:

> Look, he is coming with the clouds, and every eye will see him, even those
> who pierced him. (Revelation 1:7)

> They will see the Son of Man coming on the clouds of the sky, with power
> and great glory. (Matthew 24:30)

This climactic event, for which all creation groans, has been the
earnest expectation of succeeding generations of believers. The fact that
Christ's second advent is mentioned 318 times in the 210 chapters of
the New Testament indicates the important place it fills in the temple
of Christian truth.

Alexander Maclaren remarked that "the primitive church thought
a great deal more about the coming of Christ than about death, and
thought a great deal more about His coming than about heaven." Out
of a lifetime of scholarship, James Denney said, "We cannot call in

question what stands so plainly in the pages of the New Testament, what filled so exclusively the minds of early Christians—the idea of a personal return of Christ at the end of the age. If we are to retain any relation to the New Testament at all, we must assert the personal return of Christ as Judge of all."

It is a cause for regret, however, that this great truth, which should have been a unifying factor in the life of the church, has become the ground of heated contention between some who embrace opposing views on matters of detail, while holding the same great fact as an article of faith. In this concluding section we shall concentrate on those certainties that are shared by most to whom the advent of our Lord is a cherished hope.

WHAT IT IS NOT

Many who for various reasons are unwilling to believe that our Lord will return visibly and bodily try to explain the relevant Scriptures in one of the following ways, all of which to the author seem equally unsatisfactory in adequately interpreting these passages.

The Lord comes at death. But does He? Does not the Scripture teach rather that the believer departs to be with the Lord (Philippians 1:23)? To reveal the faults of this contention, the substitution of "death" for the Lord's coming in certain passages is a sufficient proof; for example, "[Waiting] for the blessed hope—the glorious appearing of our great God and Savior, Jesus Christ" (Titus 2:13). How does death fit into this picture?

The Lord came in the descent of the Spirit at Pentecost. There is a sense in which that was *a* coming of Christ in which they exchanged His presence for His omnipresence, but it was not the fulfillment of the many passages foretelling *the* second coming of Christ. This is shown by the fact that many statements concerning His advent were made after Pentecost (e.g., Philippians 3:20–21). Moreover, our Lord affirmed that the coming of the Spirit was dependent on His *departure,* not on His *advent* (John 7:37–39).

The Lord came at the destruction of Jerusalem. It should be noted that in the gospel passage where the fall of Jerusalem is alluded to there is no indication that it is identical to or at the same time as the Second Advent (Matthew 24:2–3). It was after the destruction of Jerusalem that John recorded these words of Jesus: "Peter . . . asked, 'Lord, what about him [John]?' Jesus answered, 'If I want him to remain alive *until I return,* what is that to you? You must follow me'" (John 21:21–22, italics added).

WHAT IT IS

The clearest statement of the nature of Christ's advent was made by the angels immediately following His ascension. "This same Jesus, who has been taken from you into heaven, will come back in the same way you have seen him go into heaven" (Acts 1:11). Commenting on this passage, Alexander Maclaren said, "He will come in like manner as He has gone. We are not to water down such words with anything short of a return precisely corresponding in its method to the departure: and as the departure was visible, corporeal, literal, personal, and local, so too will be His return from heaven to earth."

The return of the Lord will be personal. "I am coming soon" (Revelation 22:7).

It will be a literal return, since it will be "in the same way" as He went (Acts 1:11). His ascension was no mere vision but a factual event.

It will be visible. "Every eye will see him, even those who pierced him" (Revelation 1:7).

It will be glorious, for He will come "in his Father's glory" (Matthew 16:27), and in His own glory (2 Thessalonians 1:7–9), and in the glory of the angels (Matthew 25:31).

It will be a sudden appearing, like a lightning flash (Matthew 24:27).

It will be unexpected. Men will deny that He is coming, advancing as proof that "everything goes on as it has since the beginning of creation" (2 Peter 3:4). He will come "like a thief" (1 Thessalonians 5:2–3), and the advent of a thief is always unexpected. He also said He would come "at an hour when you do not expect him" (Matthew 24:44).

THE TIME OF THE ADVENT

While Scripture appears to teach that no millennium will intervene before our Lord returns to receive His redeemed ones to Himself, the actual time of that return is unrevealed. Indeed, any attempt at fixing its date is doomed to failure. It is a secret locked in the heart of the Father. Our Lord's own words were: "No one knows about that day or hour, not even the angels in heaven, nor the Son, but only the Father" (Matthew 24:36). And again: "It is not for you to know the times or seasons, which the Father hath put in his own power" (Acts 1:7 KJV).

The Bible tells us a sufficient amount to satisfy faith, although not always enough to gratify our curiosity. The New Testament was not written to satisfy the inquisitive but to glorify the One who is coming and to stimulate faith in Him. Although we may not know the exact day nor hour, the Lord indicated that we could know when His coming was at hand. The coincidence of certain signs would be its sure precursor.

There would be *a doctrinal sign*—widespread apostasy and departure from the faith (2 Thessalonians 2:3; 1 Timothy 4:1). Scoffers would ridicule the idea of His coming (2 Peter 3:3).

There would be *political signs,* days of peril nationally and socially (2 Timothy 3:1). "Nations will be in anguish and perplexity" (Luke 21:25).

There would be *a financial sign*—the great amassing of wealth. "You have hoarded wealth in the last days" (James 5:3).

There would be *a Jewish sign.* In the light of the astounding Six-Day War between Israel and the Arab world and the liberation of Jerusalem from the kind of external domination that had prevailed until then, our Lord's prediction is most significant. "Jerusalem will be trampled on by the Gentiles until the times of the Gentiles are fulfilled" (Luke 21:24). In the same discourse He referred to the budding of the fig tree— a symbol of the quickening into national life of Israel—and said, "When you see these things happening, you know that the kingdom of God is near" (Luke 21:31).

There would be *an evangelistic sign.* "And this gospel of the kingdom will be preached in the whole world as a testimony to all nations, and then the end will come" (Matthew 24:14). "The gospel must first be preached to all nations" (Mark 13:10). The great missionary activity of our day has resulted in Christianity's becoming for the first time a universal religion. There does not remain any major national group in which the church of Christ has not been established.

With the fulfillment of these signs so evidently before our eyes, we have abundant warrant for believing that "[He] is near, right at the door" (Mark 13:29).

THE SECOND ADVENT AND MISSIONS

It was rather shattering to discover that at a recent prophetic conference, among the large number of addresses delivered, not one dealt with this most important theme.

Scripture appears to teach that three things must take place before Christ returns.

The church must be ready. "The wedding of the Lamb has come, and his bride has made herself ready" (Revelation 19:7). This is not something God does; it is something for which He waits. There is no need to stress the urgency of a purifying of the church.

The church must be complete. Christ cannot and will not come for an incomplete church. Not until the last soul is won to complete the bride, the last stone laid to complete the spiritual temple, can He come. His bride is to be completely representative of humanity, for people of every kindred, tongue, tribe, and nation compose it (Revelation 7:9–10).

The church must have finished its task. But how can we know when it is completed? We cannot know, and therefore we must use every means to give the Gospel to every creature.

OUR ATTITUDE TO THE ADVENT

This doctrine is nothing if not practical in its application. There is hardly any Second Advent text in the New Testament that does not in itself or in its context insist upon the influence such a hope ought to have on our inner spiritual life or the mood of our soul.

It is set forth as *an incentive to holy living* (e.g. 1 John 2:28; 3:3). It is bound up with every practical exhortation to Christian obligation, service, and attainment—for example, patience (James 5:7–8), holiness (Titus 2:11–13), watchfulness (Mark 13:34–37). Since that is so, it is unfortunate that so much emphasis has been given by exponents of this truth to its speculative side and so little to its ethical implications.

We are exhorted to "*love* his appearing" (2 Timothy 4:8 KJV, italics added) and live in the light of it. We should *look for* His return and because of it be optimists amid the prevailing pessimism. Though we are in the midst of perilous times, more glorious days lie just ahead (2 Peter 3:12–13).

We are to *wait* and *watch* for His coming (Mark 13:35; 1 Corinthians 1:7), not in idle sloth but in earnest service. Since He may come at any moment, we must be watching every moment.

We are to "occupy" or "do business" till He comes (Luke 19:13 KJV; see NIV). This truth will not turn us into mere visionaries but will stir us to more zealous service for our Master.

As a conclusion I include statements of representative Christians testifying to the transforming effect this truth has had on their life and service as collated by Delavan L. Pierson.

EFFECT OF BELIEF IN THE SECOND ADVENT

The effect on soul winning. George Mueller testified that the effect it produced on him was this: "From my inmost soul I was stirred up to feel compassion for perishing sinners and for the slumbering world lying around us in the wicked one. Ought I not to do what I can to win souls for the sleeping church? I determined to go from place to place to preach the gospel, and arouse the church to look and wait for the second advent of our Lord from heaven. For fifty-one years my heart had been true to these two points."

The effect on hope. Wilbur Chapman, the famous evangelist, wrote:

"The truth of our Lord's premillennial return has worked out in my life in a very practical and helpful way. It has increased my desire to serve Him. It has given me an optimistic spirit concerning the advancement of the cause of Christ, and it has given me an ever-increasing joy in preaching."

The effect on faith. Anderson-Berry, of Scotland, the son of a minister, who became an atheist, wrote that one night a friend asked him to go to a religious meeting where the return of the Lord was being discussed. What he heard led to his conversion. He says, "The Lord brought me to Himself and prepared me *for* His coming by revealing to me the truth *about* His coming."

The effect on Bible study. Arthur T. Pierson, a well-known Bible scholar and missionary advocate, wrote, "When I found this truth I began to discover what I had not seen before, that it is the pivot of every epistle of the New Testament. Two-thirds of the Bible which had been sealed to me were opened by this key, and I was permitted to enter and walk through the marvellous chambers of mystery."

The effect on life. J. Hudson Taylor, founder of the China Inland Mission, wrote, "I believe that the ignorance of native Christians generally of the fact that Christ is coming again is one reason for the selfishness and the worldliness to be found in some branches of the Church in China. Well do I remember the effect when God was pleased to open my own heart to this great truth that the Lord Jesus was coming again and might come at any time. Since He may come any day, it is well to be ready every day. I do not know of any truth that has been a greater blessing to me through life than this."

The effect on service. A. J. Gordon, one of the brilliant spiritual Bible teachers and ministers of the past century, wrote, "If we believe that the renovation of the world is contingent upon the return of Christ, and that the time of His return will be determined, as far as the Church is concerned, by witnessing to the gospel of the Kingdom among all peoples, no expression of doubt as to the permanent value of missionary work among non-Christian peoples can deter us from any self-sacrifice which may hasten that consummation."

The effect on thought. The Earl of Shaftesbury, one of Great Britain's most famous Christian reformers, wrote, "I do not think that in the last forty years I have lived one conscious hour that was not influenced by the thought of the Lord's return."

The effect on preaching. O. F. Bartholow, pastor of a large church and leader of a noted men's Bible class, wrote, "I was trained in the post-millennium view, but when I began to study the Bible I came to believe in the pre-millennium view and to preach it. The result has been that a new spirit came into my preaching. It put new power and the spirit of service in the Church, and gave energy in every field of activity."

The effect on missionary motive. Arthur T. Pierson wrote, "From the first day when I saw the hope of our Lord's return as imminent, new courage came into my soul, and new iron into my blood, and I have been labouring under the divinely inspired expectation of the successful completion of Christ's body, the Church, an expectation that is confirmed and established both by experience and observation."

KEY INSIGHT
INTO THE LIFE AND WORK OF CHRIST

Christ will not return until He has finished His task of building His church, so we need to get ready as individuals and share our faith with others.

Other books by Moody Press and J. Oswald Sanders

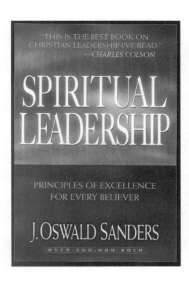

Spiritual Leadership
**Principles of Excellence
for Every Believer**

With more than 500,000 in print, *Spiritual Leadership* has proven itself a timeless classic in teaching the principles of leadership. J. Oswald Sanders presents and illustrates those principles through biographies of eminent men of God—men such as Moses, Nehemiah, Paul, David Livingstone, and Charles Spurgeon. *Spiritual Leadership* will encourage you to place your talents and powers at His disposal so you can become a leader used for His glory.

ISBN #0-8024-6799-7, Paperback

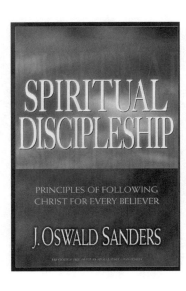

Spiritual Discipleship
**Principles of Following Christ
for Every Believer**

Most Christians desire a life that brings glory and honor to God. Yet few fully understand the absolute sacrifice that Christ asks of a true disciple. *Spiritual Discipleship* stresses the need for putting others before oneself and a recognition of Christ's lordship. This book is a must for any Christian who seeks a better under-standing of the nature of servanthood.

ISBN #0-8024-6798-9, Paperback